MY BABY CAN SLEEP

The Real Reasons Your Baby Won't Sleep;
The Quick Fixes without Breaking Your
Attachment; and the Secrets to
Predictability, Flexibility, and Joy in Parenting

Written By Brad and Greta Zude

MyBabyCanSleep.com

My Baby Can Sleep:
The Real Reasons Your Baby Won't Sleep;
The Quick Fixes Without Breaking Your Attachment; and
The Secrets to Predictability, Flexibility and Joy in Parenting

Written by Brad & Greta Zude
www.mybabycansleep.com

Edited by Kelly Lipin, Clear Message Editing & Review

Copyright © 2019 My Baby Can Sleep, Inc.
ISBN 978-1-7327-219-0-6
First Edition
Printed in the USA

To Cal and Brenda, where it all began;
and to our children, who forced us to become experts.

"Behold, children are a heritage from the Lord,
the fruit of the womb is a reward."

Psalm 127:3

TABLE OF CONTENTS

Here's your ticket into our online community:

MyBabyCanSleep.com/BookGroup

INTRODUCTION

So, your baby isn't sleeping, huh? Well, you are not alone. Many moms and dads have little ones who won't sleep through the night. I say "won't" because it is not that your baby can't sleep through the night. You might feel that way, but let me encourage you: Your baby can sleep. Your baby will sleep. My husband, Brad, and I (Greta) are here to help.

You picked up this book for one or more of many possible reasons. You are pregnant with your first child and you have heard horror stories from your friends who've had babies who just won't sleep through the night. You are pregnant with another child; your first child took forever to sleep through the night; and you are determined to make things different this time around. Or, you are currently stuck in the cycle of sleepless nights with your infant. Frustrated and tired, you think you have forgotten what a good night's sleep feels like. Maybe you want your bed back—a bed that has been commandeered by your baby.

Regardless of your reasons for reading this book, I want to congratulate you for taking this step.

REMEMBER WHEN?

Do you remember date nights with your spouse? Do you remember what it was like to enjoy an evening on the couch watching an entire movie, uninterrupted by trips to your baby's crib or bed? Do you remember waking up in the morning feeling rested, energetic, and ready for the day ahead? No?

I am not trying to rub salt in an open wound. We understand. We've been there. We know how difficult it can be to have a baby struggling to sleep, whether your sleepless baby is your first child or your seventh (like us). The good news is there are answers to the problem. There is hope! Your life doesn't have to be this way anymore.

Imagine not feeling the stress (or even fear) that comes with anticipating a sleepless night. Imagine waking up rested and ready to take on the day. You can have your life back. You can return to enjoying date nights and quiet evenings with your spouse. Oh, and you can even put your baby down at a friend's house without completely embarrassing yourself!

Brad and I are going to take you through an amazing system that is taking the "baby sleep" world by storm. It is a system that is helping moms, dads, and families around the world to live a "MyBabyCanSleep" lifestyle.

AN HONEST EVALUATION

Before we continue, we want you to take a self-examination and ask yourself a few questions. The reason for this brief evaluation is that our experience tells us you are likely considering some things as you begin this book: Do I really want to do this? Is the solution going to be more painful than the problem? Is it easier to just endure the frustration and exhaustion? After all, this can't last forever, right? It is possible that evaluating your current circumstances is just the motivation you need to make those challenging but necessary steps.

In order to honestly assess your situation, ask yourself the following questions:

- Do I have other children who have needs? Are their needs being met?
- Are my struggling baby's sleep and developmental needs being met by what I'm doing now?
- What about my spouse? Are my spouse's needs being met?
- What about my responsibilities in managing my home? If things continue as they are, am I meeting those responsibilities?
- There is life outside my home—At least there is supposed to be. Is my baby's sleeplessness negatively impacting relationships with my extended family,

friends and community?

- And what about me? What is my baby's sleeplessness doing to me physically and mentally? Am I being selfish by simply wanting to be well?

Brad and I are confident that we know how you answered the questions. Why? Because we've been there, and because we have helped many people who also answered these questions honestly.

We understand that, as human beings, we are all imperfect. Show us a person who thinks they perfectly fulfill all of their obligations, and we will show you a person who could be the subject of another book called "The Delusion of Perfection." However, mature people, loving and caring people—people like you—are characterized by a desire to meet the needs identified in the above self-evaluation.

Our hope is that this evaluation has added some important perspective to your thinking. What you have tried, or what you are doing now to help your baby sleep isn't working. Your baby's sleeplessness is affecting your baby's well-being, your own well-being, and the well-being of your family. That's why you have picked up this book. Yes, it will be hard at times. Again, we understand. But you know, as the self-evaluation showed you, it is time to turn the corner. It's time for your baby to learn the skill of sleep.

WHAT IS SLEEP TRAINING?

You know there is a problem, but what is the solution? Sleep training! Sleep training is teaching your baby the skill of sleep. Putting yourself to sleep and remaining asleep is actually a skill that we need to learn. Sleep training teaches this skill without the aid of associations and crutches (i.e. rocking, bouncing, nursing, singing, reading, etc.). Sleep training is not just for babies five months and older, either. A two-week-old baby can be taught healthy sleep habits as well! While they won't be sleeping through an entire 12-hour night without a feeding, we can start even the youngest babies on the right path. Then when they are ready to go without a feeding at night, it will happen effortlessly. Sleep training enables your baby to sleep in an age-appropriate way, ideal for their current stage of development.

Sleep training does bring a stigma along with it and in this book, we will address the elephant in the room: the fear of any possible neglect or unintentional harm to your baby in your efforts to break the habits and cycle of sleeplessness. You have put your baby to bed. Your baby begins to cry. The natural, loving attachment you have to your child now has you crying too. You want your baby to sleep, but you don't want your baby to cry. It is tempting to skip right to chapter three, but please don't! Bear with us as we discuss other parenting methods and how they just don't seem to fulfill the needs of the whole family.

OTHER THEORIES ARE BABY-CENTERED

Most theories that attempt to solve the problem of a sleepless baby are baby-centered. Is that bad?

One method, known as "attachment parenting," claims to promote attachment between baby and parent. This is attachment is achieved by the parent responding immediately to every cry, making the bed available for co-sleeping, wearing baby, and feeding on demand. This method uses fear and guilt to make parents think their baby will be emotionally or physically harmed by giving the baby independence, or by letting the baby learn to sleep.

Sadly, the result of this methodology is that a parent's world (most often mom's) is completely centered around the baby's—and only the baby's—needs. Catering to a baby's every need, whether real or perceived, especially during the baby's first year of life, can result in negative, even tragic, consequences. Possible consequences include, but are not limited to:

- Neglect of mother's health and well-being
- Neglect of the marital relationship
- Neglect of the needs of other children
- Resentment toward the baby
- Resentment toward the baby and the parents by other children in the home
- Neglect of the care of the home

- Neglect of relationships outside the immediate family, including: extended family, friends, church, and community

HARMFUL EFFECTS OF SLEEP DEPRIVATION

Some governments and their various agencies use sleep deprivation as a form of torture. Needless to say, sleep deprivation can negatively impact the health and well-being of both baby and parents. Sleep deprivation in a baby can result in:

- Noted lack of interest in people and the immediate environment
- Tendency to look away from things that ought to stimulate the baby
- Becoming more accident prone
- Becoming clingier and less independent
- Possible developmental delays

For parents, sleep deprivation can result in:

- Increased injuries, accidents, and sick days
- Postpartum depression and postpartum anxiety
- Diminished cognitive processes, including: impaired attention, alertness, concentration, reasoning, memory, and problem solving

- Health issues, such as: heart disease, heart attack, heart failure, irregular heartbeat, high blood pressure, stroke, and diabetes
- Increased symptoms of depression and anxiety
- Weight gain

The human body is designed in such a way that sleep is required for health and proper function. Getting your baby to sleep will benefit the emotional and physical health of baby and the entire family.

Additionally, a sleeping baby who is trained and disciplined to do what comes naturally, promotes a healthy family structure.

FAMILY STRUCTURE

As stated already, one of the responsibilities of every individual, including moms, is fostering and maintaining healthy relationships. Without minimizing or marginalizing the importance of single mothers, there is no relationship more critical to a healthy family structure than the relationship between husband and wife—father and mother. An imbalance between meeting the needs of a sleepless baby and the needs of the rest of the family can negatively impact this most important familial relationship.

It bears stating again that a sleepless baby, and employing wrong methods to solve the problem, often results in a reduction or even an elimination of private time between husband and wife. Dates are a thing of the past because babysitters are unable to watch your children beyond bedtime.

A sleepless baby turns the marriage into the family bed. The husband/wife relationship is the glue that keeps the family together. If this foundation is damaged, your children have no firm, familial relationship setting the tone and direction for all of family life.

IT'S HARD WORK, BUT NOT SLAVERY

Unfortunately, many people think the process involved in training a baby to sleep is so cumbersome and time consuming that you lose all flexibility and every form of freedom. Nothing could be further from the truth. A routine, even the routine of getting your baby to sleep, allows for more life planning; not less. With a disciplined structure, you can plan your day and night around your baby's sleep training. You will miss fewer events, meetings, and appointments by scheduling around the best time(s) of day for your baby.

A FINAL WORD BEFORE WE GET TO WORK

With all of this in mind, it's almost time to begin a new journey, a better journey. It's almost time to get to work—to get your baby to sleep. I've already congratulated you for picking up this book. I'm guessing you expect me, as the author, to do that. But I want you to know how much Brad and I care about you, the reader—the mom, the dad, the parent. And we love your children. We want your babies to sleep because we love you and because we love your kids. Our lives, which we will share with you in greater detail in Chapter One, have been drastically impacted by this sleep training for babies. We've progressed from desperate parents, to wary participants, to blessed beneficiaries, to excited advocates, to motivated and committed counselors and trainers.

Brad and I are all in. Our babies sleep. Our students around the world now have babies who sleep. And your baby will sleep.

Let's start by showing you what we never would have imagined ten years ago.

Chapter One

OUR STORY

Whether you stumbled upon our book in a frantic search for something to help get your baby to sleep, or a friend recommended us to you, you're probably wondering who we are. *"What's their story? How hard was it for them? Did I read that correctly—seven kids? What have they experienced that would lead them to become sleep consultants?"*

Before we get into the nuts and bolts of baby sleep training, let me tell you the story of how we accidentally discovered the "secret sauce" of sleep success, and how our system has gone on to affect thousands of lives around the world. Brad and I know that no two babies, no two families, no two situations are identical. So, you will likely read some things and nod your head, thinking, *"Yep, been there; done that."* You may also read parts of our story and think, *"Wow, glad I haven't made that mistake."* Or, maybe even, *"Do these two wear capes?"*

I'm going to share our story with the hope that, regardless of your present situation, you will find encouragement and even more confidence to stick with us and let us help you get your baby sleeping.

Our journey began before our first child was even a thought in our minds.

Friends of ours at church were teaching a parenting class. One day, they asked us if we would like to attend their next class. Brad and I thought about it and agreed it would be a good idea. Although we did not yet have children, we wanted to be prepared for parenting when the time came. We wanted to be different. We wanted to be ahead of the game and avoid the baby horror stories we heard so much about. It was important to us that we applied godly principles in the raising of our children, from the beginning of their lives. So, there we were…awkwardly the ONLY couple in the course without children, (not even pregnant yet), we joined the class.

As the Lord would have it, we learned we were expecting our first child while attending the parenting class! We were motivated before we learned we were pregnant. Now, our motivation was at a much higher level. Things suddenly got very real for us.

We were all in. We tried to absorb as much information as we possibly could. I'll be honest; we were a bit arrogant, prideful, and maybe naïve. Brad and I were going to be the smartest parents. I was valedictorian of my high school. Brad and I both had degrees from the University of Iowa. We were over-achievers that were going to figure everything out *before* our daughter arrived. We were determined not to be "those" parents with one of "those" kids who wouldn't sleep through the night.

Brad and I were certain we would be trailblazers in getting our baby to sleep, even though we were still several months away from experiencing our first night with a baby in our home. We read all the books available at the time. We formulated plans. I even had a spreadsheet. We were going to be an unstoppable, parental force—a force against which no stubborn baby would stand a sleepless chance.

Our friends gently tried to bring some perspective to our thinking. "Your baby will set your schedule," they said. "You won't set your baby's schedule." We would have none of it. We appreciated the counsel and the heart behind it, but we were determined to be different. Our parenting would be different. Our baby would be different. Zude Baby #1 was going to sleep well.

> We were going to be an unstoppable, parental force—a force against which no stubborn baby would stand a sleepless chance.

Our little girl, Annika, was born. For the first four weeks of

3

her life, everything went just as Brad and I planned. I swaddled little Annika, place her in her crib, and she would nap like a perfect little baby. I remember watching her sleep and smugly thinking, *"Yep. I've got this all figured out."* And the proof was in my bundled-up, pretty little cup of pudding.

Annika quickly began to extend her nights' sleep. Not even a month old, and our baby was already sleeping six hours a night. Life with baby was perfect.

Then it happened—what I refer to in my home as "The Four-Week Curse."

Annika no longer wanted to sleep. Often with tears and sometimes wailing, she now refused to take naps. She went from sleeping most of the night to refusing to fall asleep until about 1:00 am. And there I sat in the chair next to her swing, holding the pacifier in her mouth, desperately trying to get her to sleep, all-the-while wondering (while slipping in and out of semi-consciousness), if I would ever sleep well again.

Then there was Brad. *That man.* My husband. I started getting angry with him. "I just want you to help me! Get up with me to feed the baby!" Poor Brad; he couldn't do anything. I was breastfeeding, so he couldn't feed the baby. And he had to go to work in the morning. He needed sleep, too.

The exhausting, sometimes vicious sleepless cycle had begun. I was grumpy with Brad. In turn, he was grumpy with me. We were frustrated with our baby. Our situation grew desperate.

Brad and I started fighting about solutions. We couldn't agree, and we had become what we determined we wouldn't become. We were now "those" parents, with one of "those" babies. Seemingly overnight, we went from new parents who thought we had it all figured out, to parents, like so many others, who didn't have a clue about how to get our baby to sleep. We went from priding ourselves as parents to whom other parents should turn for help, to new parents that now needed help ourselves.

> We were now faced with the painful reality that our plan had failed.

Brad and I had studied for almost a year. The result: a plan in which we had a great deal of confidence. However, we were now faced with the painful reality that our plan had failed. In hindsight, we realized that in all of our planning we didn't take into account the emotional stress that would come if our baby couldn't sleep. What we didn't consider possible, even in theory, we were now experiencing in reality: frustration, hopelessness, defeat.

Brad and I were so tired and so stressed-out, and obviously too close to the situation (it couldn't be any more personal), to see a way out. There's a reason why lawyers don't represent their own families in court. There's a reason why surgeons don't operate on their own spouses or children. It's just too personal for them to see and think clearly—to be objective. We couldn't see a light at the end of the tunnel because we weren't looking for it. We were too consumed with pounding our heads against the wall of the darkened tunnel to see so much as a ray of hope on the other side. Our emotional state made us unable to access the abundant knowledge we had gathered.

The first step we took was a difficult one. Although embarrassed to do so (after all, we had a plan and we had let everyone know it), we reached out. We decided to turn to our mentor for help. Since she had been out of the "baby sleep" game for many years, she put us in touch with a sleep consultant.

It was wonderful! Through that process, the sleep consultant helped us to see the forest for the trees. She held our hand, so to speak, and asked good questions—the *right* questions. She got to know our baby and our specific situation. She re-assured us that everything was going to be fine, and that we'd get through it. Then she helped us fix our specific problems.

Within two weeks, Annika was back to taking amazing naps. Our baby was sleeping again! We put her down for bed with ease at 7:30 pm, not 1:00 am. By seven weeks of age, she was accomplishing almost a full night's sleep. In fact, it was at the eight-week mark that Annika began to sleep through the entire night, with one small feeding before I retired around 10:00 pm.

Through that process, which, at times resembled an emotional roller coaster, we became fascinated with "baby sleep" and how to accomplish it—how to get a baby on a routine; how to train a baby to sleep on his or her own.

Now, it wasn't as simple as setting a schedule, sticking to it, and putting my baby down to sleep. It did take work. It did take a lot of learning and re-learning on our part. But Brad and I were fully committed to collecting and applying as much good information as possible. We experienced a baby who wouldn't sleep. We experienced the frustration of trying and failing to get our baby to sleep. We experienced the humbling process of admitting we didn't have it all figured out, and then asking for help. And, thankfully, we experienced the euphoria of a peacefully sleeping baby once again.

Before long, people who had followed our sleepless journey started asking us questions. They wanted to know exactly how we got Annika sleeping again. We started teaching what we had learned to our friends, family members, and even strangers who reached out to us. The strangers were coming to us via word-of-mouth, as people we had helped were telling their friends, who told their friends, and so on. People wanted and needed help, and we were more than eager to give it to them. We had soon realized that good information and schedules

> We experienced the euphoria of a peacefully sleeping baby once again.

paired with ongoing support was not only hard to find, but outrageously expensive to obtain with a consultant.

Through the process of experiencing failure, training, and success with our own children, as well as the additional experience of helping others, Brad and I realized we had developed an amazingly unique system that was more than what a book could supply. Along the way, we discovered that this strategy, these principles, are effective in getting *any* baby to sleep (regardless of where the baby is developmentally). The results have been nothing short of amazing. We've seen babies in our own family, and many other families, go from utter sleeplessness to consistent full night of sleep and great day time naps.

Of course, there were skeptics along the way. "You're just lucky," some people said. But after baby number two, three, four, and five, even the skeptics were admitting the obvious. Our strategy to help our babies (and the babies of other parents) worked. Our formula for baby sleep was tried, tested, and produced results—*good* results.

Brad and I remember the time we spent preparing to help our baby sleep, before our baby was born. This is why we are committed to helping not only the parents of children who are sleeping (or supposed to be sleeping) in cribs and beds, but also the parents of children who are yet in the womb. We are also ready and able to help the parents of older children, three years old and beyond.

Now, let's fast-forward to the days following the birth of our sixth child. Brad, my sweet husband whom I dearly love, has always had an entrepreneurial spirit. He came home one day, about two weeks after our son, John-Luke, was born and declared, "I've got it!" he said. "I know what our next business is going to be! We're going to be baby sleep consultants! We know how to do this. This is what we're really good at. And we're going to get our information out to the masses."

He decided we needed to share our ongoing mentorship model with as many people as possible. Especially since we could offer a continuous premium service for the same amount or less than what most consultants charge for a one-hour phone call! We'd be able to stick with our students just like our consultant did with us. We realized that the amount of information you have isn't nearly as relevant as your ability to execute what needs to be done during a time of deep stress. That's how what we did became so different.

Brad and I immediately turned this information + support model into our full blown Sleep Accelerator Course (which we will tell you more about later) to work with moms and dads to get their babies sleeping, and became virtual consultants for baby sleep. We believed it was our obligation to make our three-tiered model (which we developed almost by accident during our period of no sleep) available to parents around the world. Next we recorded a promotional video called "The Three Secrets of a Sleeping Baby." We posted it to Facebook and it was viewed millions of times. Little did we know what would happen next….

Before we knew it, Brad and I were doing interviews on radio and other media formats all over the world! *Pregnancy and Newborn* magazine and *Romper.com* featured us as "sleep experts." Now, almost two years later, we have surpassed the 1,000-family mark in our Sleep Accelerator Course. I think it's safe to say that our work is going viral.

While we hope our story has encouraged you and motivated you to continue in the all-important process of getting your baby to sleep, enough about us. Let's talk about you. After all, we've written this book for you and your baby. We want this to be your success story, just like the amazing testimonials you will see at the end of each chapter.

First things first. You might currently find yourself stuck in a hole you've dug, perhaps unintentionally. In the next chapter, we'll identify exactly where you are, and help you stop digging deeper. If you are expecting a baby, we will show you how to avoid the hole entirely!

Angela Hardt
7 mins · ⚙

Life changing & amazing sums up **#mybabycansleep**! New parents here to beautiful TRIPLETS! Yes, 3 newborns at once. One night in sleepless desperation we came across Brad & Greta's program. In 2 nights we were sleeping thru the night with no sleep crutches! AMAZING🙌

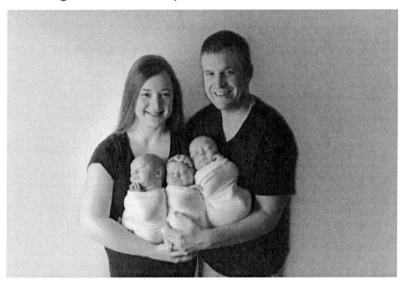

👍 Like   💬 Comment

Aubrey Carlson
1 hour ago · 🖼

The overwhelm of being new parents mixed with conflicting advice from family and friends led us to completely guessing with our daughter's sleep needs! We were fortunate to find MBCS when our daughter was just a few weeks old. We implemented the principles at 6 weeks, and she was sleeping 8 hours overnight at 8 weeks, 12 hours by 12 weeks, and is a great napper and nighttime sleeper to this day at 1 year. We're so thankful for the routine, knowledge, structure and sleep that MBCS gave our family! — with **Alex Carlson**.

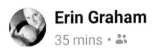

Erin Graham
35 mins · 👥

⋯

Life with 2 Two and under is crazy to say the least at times but if there is one thing that has made our lives easier is Mybabycansleep. There are so many things that I am thankful for with this course, our favorite is having a baby sleeping through the night since 8 weeks old! The second best thing that **Brad Zude** and Greta taught us was how to keep a schedule and routine for our family. Our favorite part of having a schedule is since Levi was born the boys have been able to nap and go to bed at the same time!

👍 Like   💬 Comment   ↪ Share

Chapter Two

STOP DIGGING

If you're reading this book, you are likely asking yourself a series of questions. They probably go something like this: "How did we get here? How did we come to this place of pure and complete exhaustion? Our baby is one month old; ten months old; two years old—Why are we stuck in this hole and still not sleeping through the night?"

Even though it's discouraging, you can't help but admit the obvious like Brad and I did. "Since we're not sleeping, I'm a grump; my baby is a grump; my spouse is a grump. We are not happy. We can hardly stand each other, anymore. If we could just get some decent sleep!"

In this chapter, we will focus our attention on answering the question, "How did we get here?" We will accomplish this by addressing the more common causes of a sleepless baby (and family): feeding philosophy, a chaotic metabolism, and sleep crutches. Most people do not realize that the way we feed our babies and the way we think about their feeding needs actually determine how well (or poorly) our babies sleep during the night and during the day.

FEEDING PHILOSOPHY:
CRYING DOESN'T ALWAYS MEAN HUNGRY

The predominant feeding philosophy of our day, and therefore, the way most parents go about feeding their babies, is to simply feed them whenever they act as though they are hungry. A baby's communication is limited to crying to express want or need. Since feeding often stops a baby from crying, parents assume that a baby is hungry whenever he or she cries. This is not necessarily the case.

More often than not, what parents identify as hunger cues are something else entirely. Many times baby cries because he or she is tired, not because he or she is hungry. Even rooting or sucking, in newborns, can simply be a natural reflex response, not necessarily a hunger cue. Just because a baby seems to be looking for the breast or the bottle doesn't automatically mean the baby is hungry. Yes, babies do root and suck when they are hungry. However, many times they are trying to comfort themselves to sleep and just need to be put to bed. They don't constantly need their tummies stuffed.

Responding to your baby's rooting and sucking by feeding

them conditions your baby to need food to sleep. Food literally becomes a sleep crutch. More about this in a minute.

Responding to your baby's cries with food can also result in smaller daytime feedings. The result: babies never actually fill their tummies or satisfy their hunger. Shorter feedings result in babies only receiving *foremilk*, which has fewer nutrients and lesser fat density than *hindmilk*. This diminishes the baby's ability to sustain themselves, while awake or asleep, for appropriate periods of time.

> Just because a baby seems to be looking for the breast or bottle doesn't automatically mean the baby is hungry.

Feeding on-demand also leads to erratic feedings. It prevents a baby from getting into a consistent feeding and sleeping rhythm. Our bodies are habit-driven. We quickly and easily establish patterns in life. We each tend to wake up at the same time every morning. We need that first cup of coffee by a certain time. We eat at about the same times each day. We turn in at about the same time each night. We drive the same way to work every day. We likely start down the same aisle to begin our shopping trips. We are, by nature, creatures of habit. Our babies are very easily, for better or for worse, trained to be the same way. Unfortunately, old habits are hard to break, and doing all this by yourself is the hardest possible route to take. We'll touch more on this in chapters nine and ten.

QUICK SIDE NOTE: REFLUX

If your baby struggles with reflux, feeding your baby on-demand might be pouring gasoline on a fire. If your baby is struggling to keep milk down, and you are continually demand feeding your baby, the end result might be an increase in acid in your baby's sensitive and growing digestive system. Babies tend to be grumpier (not less grumpy), when they vomit. Your baby is not hungry, but you are feeding him. Your baby is gassy, and by demand feeding your baby, you might be causing an increase in your baby's gas levels. Your baby's body wants to expel milk while, at the same time, you are forcing more milk down the same pipe, creating a vicious cycle of an uncomfortable and discontent baby.

We have worked with hundreds of families all over the world whose babies' reflux all but disappeared when they stopped demand feeding their babies. Certainly, babies still spit-up. After all, that's what babies do. But the frequent projectile vomiting associated with reflux is diminished greatly when demand feeding is replaced with a stable, manageable feeding routine.

ERRATIC FEEDINGS AND CHAOTIC METABOLISM

Since demand feeding times are inconsistent by nature, your baby's feeding times will be erratic, day and night. Your baby doesn't know how to stabilize their own metabolism, nor how to create healthy eating and sleeping habits for necessary consistency in his or her schedule. Maybe your baby wants to snack-feed all night long. As a result, your baby is up throughout the night, catching second wind after second wind. Or your baby, so exhausted from a sleepless night, just wants to sleep all day. What your baby does not understand is that he or she is simply tired--exhausted. So, your baby cries and it becomes a vicious cycle for baby, for mom and dad, for the whole family.

This was the situation with one of our students named Chantelle. When she came to us, she was feeding her baby on-demand. Her baby would wake 10-20 times every night. When the baby would wake, Chantelle would nurse to try to put her back to sleep. She would do this over and over again, throughout the night. Imagine how exhausted Chantelle was after just one night like this, let alone weeks on end!

Within three nights of helping Chantelle to establish a manageable and consistent schedule, her baby was sleeping through the night.

The way we think about feeding our children impacts and determines the way our children sleep.

SLEEP CRUTCHES

Earlier I mentioned something I refer to as "sleep crutches." What are they? Well, they are the tactics that tired parents end up using, out of desperation, to get their babies to sleep. You are so exhausted, it becomes a near hostage negotiation with baby, and you begin to do things you swear you'd never do. Soon enough you've got a hot mess on your hands.

A "sleep crutch" is anything a baby associates with sleep (other than simply lying down and closing the eyes). Anything the baby has convinced himself (or herself) he needs to be able to sleep is considered a crutch. We've already discussed the most common sleep crutch: feeding on-demand. However, there are many others. Sleep crutches can include: rocking, swings, pacifiers, car rides, noise machines, and more.

One of our students, Kristine, initially had no trouble getting her baby to sleep. Up until about the three-month mark, it only took Kristine about five minutes to put her baby to sleep. However, as her baby developed, the baby's response to what Kristine did to get her to sleep changed, too.

> Sleep crutches can include: rocking, swings, pacifiers, car rides, noise machines, and more.

It got to the point where Kristine would spend up to four hours rocking, bouncing, nursing— doing whatever she could just to get her baby down to sleep at night. *Four. Hours. Every. Single. Night!* The result: only a couple hours of sleep for mommy and baby, before they started the exhausting, discouraging process all over again. They spent more time trying to get baby to sleep than actually sleeping!

Oh, how we wish we could have helped our friends, Tony and Mahria, 30 years ago. When we told them about our work as baby sleep consultants, they told us about the sleep crutch they used with their first child. The only way they could get her to sleep was to lay next to her in bed and let her run her fingers through their hair. They did this every night for more than a year! Crazy!

The important thing to remember about sleep crutches is this: what might work tonight, might not work next week. As your baby changes, so too will the effectiveness of the sleep crutches you use. Unfortunately, instead of getting rid of sleep crutches altogether, many parents turn to new crutches when the old ones stop working. Meanwhile, their babies, instead of learning to healthily and soundly sleep on their own, they wrongly learn that crutches are a necessity in life.

Sadder still is when parents dig themselves deeper and deeper into a "whatever works" philosophy. There's an old saying that goes something like this: "if you want to get out of a hole you've dug for yourself, the first step is to *stop digging*. Look, we understand. Parents don't set out intending to establish bad habits in their lives or the lives of their children. You didn't. Brad and I didn't. You just want your baby to sleep. But applying an "if it ain't broke, don't fix it" philosophy to sleep crutches is, in a sense, putting a band-aid on a mortal wound. Some of you know this because you intended to not feed on-demand or use sleep crutches, but found yourself deep into some (or both). For some of you, using and doing those things was your core game plan from the start. Either way, sleep crutches, by their very nature, are "broke" to begin with. So, they will never truly or permanently fix your baby's sleeping problems.

I also want you to consider this: Satisfaction that is based on receiving things we want never lasts. That which satisfies us now will, in time, lose either its attractiveness or effectiveness. We will begin to desire either more of what we find satisfying, or we will begin looking for something new, something different that we think will satisfy us more. It's a dark word picture, but the drug addict operates by the same satisfaction-driven mentality. The dose of a drug that at first provided the desired effect is soon increased to provide either more of the same or a better effect. When a particular drug no longer provides the desired results, a different drug is pursued.

TRAINING IN THE NEGATIVE

If adults turn to crutches in life, is it any wonder that our babies, made of the same human cloth, also desire crutches? Introducing crutches to our babies, especially when it comes to their sleep, will only result in them wanting more. This is what Brad and I call "training in the negative," which means to practice or continue doing what you don't want to have happen. For example, a basketball team would never practice *missing* their free-throws. They train in the positive and practice *making* their free-throws. Worse yet, the typical consequences of training in the negative is a perpetuated and deeper need for the thing you don't want to have happen, like every time you rock baby to sleep, they get more and more accustomed to it.

This may surprise you, especially if at first, your baby slept well. Training in the negative actually begins shortly after birth. But it's not us, the parents, who are doing the training. We are in fact, being trained by our babies. And our babies know what works: "I cry; mom feeds."

> We are in fact, being trained by our babies. And our babies know what works: "I cry; mom feeds."

It all seems very harmless, at first. After all, how manipulative can a baby whose age is determined by days and weeks, really be? Babies are born pragmatists. They do whatever works. As your baby grows, he or she will cry longer and harder to get what they want—until mom or dad gives in to his or her demands. As a result, parents (usually moms) find themselves in the unwanted places of holding their babies all day long, or sleeping with their babies instead of their husbands.

Does any or all of this sound familiar? Are you in this place, right now? Have you dug a hole so deep it seems like there's no way out? Well, *stop digging!* And be encouraged. We're going to throw you a rope, now, and help you climb out.

The first rung on the rope ladder that will lead you out of the hole of sleepless nights is dealing with a parent's biggest fear. What is it?

Turn the page.

CHAPTER 2
TAKE AWAYS

- How did you get here? Your circumstances have likely been determined by your feeding philosophy, your baby's chaotic metabolism, and the crutches you have used to get baby sleeping.

- Feeding Philosophy: Crying doesn't always indicate hunger. Many times we misinterpret a baby's cry for their desire to eat, and inadvertently create a habit for baby.

- Chaotic Metabolism: Demand feeding is inconsistent in nature and leads to a habit of snack feeding, day and night.

- Sleep Crutches: These are the things baby associates with sleep like rocking, bouncing, feeding, pacifiers, etc. When baby needs this association to accomplish sleep, a parent becomes a slave to providing this association for baby.

Brandi McMyne   · · ·

· 1 hour ago · 🖼

Sleep crutches.... Those things you do to get your baby to sleep because it's the only thing you know how to do. We did it all! Rocking, bouncing, walking, feeding to sleep (all for only a few hours of sleep) and we were beyond exhausted.
#MyBabyCanSleep helped us break those habits in mere days- and we finally got our life back... with a happy well rested baby! Without them, I'm not sure where we'd be! Thank you MBCS! 🩶

Danielle Wood
10:47pm · 🌐

When we first joined the My Baby Can Sleep, our schedule was mostly guess work and advice from our parents. We were still rocking all of our children to sleep, and barely sleeping ourselves. Now the children are sleeping through the night thanks to My Baby Can Sleep.

👍 Like   💬 Comment   ↪ Share

Grace Phillips is 😌 feeling rested.   · · ·

6 hrs · 👥

Pacifier dances, ninja nursing sessions, & constant nighttime wakings are things of the past for this family of four thanks to Mybabycansleep and their revolutionary sleep program ₂ᶻᶻ 😴 **#2under2 #byebyesleepcrutches**

👍❤️ 15

Chapter Three

A PARENT'S BIGGEST FEAR

Okay. Are you ready to finally address the elephant in the room? And what is the elephant in the room? *Crying*. We speak with hundreds of moms, dads, and families every single week and typically find that parents' biggest fear, when it comes to getting their babies to sleep, is hearing their baby cry. Worst still: hearing their babies cry and doing nothing about it.

We've all heard it said (and maybe you've heard it said by people you truly trust) that it is harmful to your baby to let them cry. It will ruin the natural attachment between baby and mom. If you let your baby cry, your baby will grow to be an anxious and fearful person. Letting your baby cry at night could lead to your child having aggression issues. As a result of these well-intended, but inaccurate warnings, some parents will go to the extreme of never letting their baby cry. Never. How exhausting! More logically... how is that even possible?

Where does this belief that you shouldn't allow your baby to cry himself to sleep come from? Here's a little background on crying.

"THE STUDY"

Maybe you've heard of the "stress hormone" your body produces when you cry. The hormone is called cortisol. It is believed by some that when large levels of cortisol remain in the human body, for prolonged periods of time, brain damage can occur. And who wants that? Who wants brain damage for themselves or for their baby?

Most "anti"-sleep trainers will cite an isolated and unfortunate study from a Romanian orphanage to support this claim. The study found that these neglected and traumatized orphans, left repeatedly unattended to cry for hours, *without basic physical and emotional needs being met*, developed various forms and degrees of brain damage. While it makes sense that babies living under such adverse conditions might develop some sort of brain abnormality, we're going to show you how to first and foremost meet your baby's needs, both physically and emotionally, and provide a loving and nurturing home while teaching them the skill of sleep. You will see that sleep training that includes allowing your baby to cry for controlled periods of time will not hurt your baby and will not make you a monstrous parent. Crying is normal, natural, and often times necessary to teach baby to bridge REM sleep cycles (more on this later). It's how God, in His infinite wisdom, designed babies. Your baby is going to be okay, and so will you, and we're going to prove it to you in this chapter!

THE OBVIOUS: BABIES CRY

Let's begin with obvious: Babies cry. Every baby cries. They cry for many reasons, and sometimes they cry for no reason at all. Remember, a baby's ability to communicate is extremely limited. If you take a toy from a baby, the baby might cry. If a baby is startled, the baby might cry. Hungry babies cry. Tired babies cry. Angry babies cry. Scared babies cry. Teething babies cry. Babies cry. We can all agree on this, yes?

However, have you ever considered this, especially as it pertains to your baby crying (instead of sleeping) at night? Have you ever considered redirecting your attention from stopping your baby's crying to allowing your baby's crying to work for you? At MyBabyCanSleep, we call this "building cry equity."

CRY EQUITY

Who among us hasn't had a grumpy baby because our baby is tired? When babies are tired they can be very grumpy and they communicate their displeasure the only way they know how—they cry. The key: making our baby's crying work for us instead of against us.

It's not rocket science...whether you're two months old or 32 years old, lack of sleep makes you grumpy! Once we teach our babies the skill of sleep, they are going to be far less grumpy. And you will be, too! Of course, there will still be times when your baby is grumpy—like all of us. What I'm going to teach you is how to make your baby's crying (because of fatigue) work for you, instead of against you.

"Cry equity" is simply a concept that means having the *crying your baby does anyway* build toward learning the skill of sleep, instead of just being a random cry because they are tired and grumpy. It's kind of like buying vs. renting a house. On the one hand, when you rent a house you are paying your rent and will never see that money again. Beyond having a roof over your head for the next month, there is no return on your investment. On the other hand, when you buy a house, with each payment and with the passing of time, you are building equity.

> Cry equity: Having the crying your baby does anyway build toward learning the skill of sleep.

This same concept applies to your baby's tears. Crying is going to happen anyway, so we might as well put it to work for you so baby can be done crying quickly. The biggest fail would be to let your baby cry for no specific reason or with no plan in place.

So, let's take a moment to think logically. What would you

prefer: having your baby cry under your supervision for controlled durations over a short period of time (as they go through the sleep training process), or having a baby that is continually fussing, crying, and miserable at night and naptime for six months—maybe a year or more—because your baby has never learned to put himself (or herself) to sleep? Of course, you want the former (less crying). Well, in order to get your baby to cry less and sleep more, you are going to have to let your baby cry some. In order to teach your baby get the rest they need, which will result in a lot less crying, you need to build cry equity from your baby's tears.

GOOD WAYS AND BAD WAYS TO LET YOUR BABY CRY

There are good ways and bad ways to let your baby cry. One bad way to let your baby cry is ignoring the very real needs of your child. Putting your baby to bed, turning off the light, and closing the door, and then ignoring your baby's need for food or a diaper change is not training your child to sleep; it's neglecting your child. Of course, Brad and I would never condone or encourage neglect. Sleep training begins *after* making sure your babies real needs have been met.

In addition to making sure your baby has been fed and has a clean diaper, you also want to make sure that his emotional needs have been met. Hold your baby. Hug your baby. Talk and sing (not to sleep) to your baby; communicate to and with your baby. Play with your baby. Even little ones have energy to burn. And make sure your baby has a consistent schedule for sleep and feeding. We'll talk more about these important aspects of preparing your baby to sleep train in the coming chapters.

Babies, as part of their inherent human nature, have the *ability* to sleep. We have all seen newborn babies that are extremely sleepy. They can go to sleep very easily. However, they don't know how to *put* themselves to sleep. This is a skill, like any other skill, that needs to be taught and learned. You can teach your baby to sleep while, at the same time, showing your baby even more love.

> Babies have the *ability* to sleep... However, they don't know how to *put* themselves to sleep.

Many people think teaching your baby to sleep and showing love for your baby are mutually exclusive activities. "My baby feels loved." Or, "I'm going to teach my baby how to sleep." In reality, they're not mutually exclusive activities. They are complimentary activities. Teaching your baby to sleep on his own is a very loving thing to do.

Most moms think spending hours rocking their babies to sleep is something that builds attachment between mother and child. However, it's not the *quantity* of time a mom spends with her baby that establishes attachment. It's the *quality* of the time spent together that establishes attachment. Moms establish stronger bonds with their babies when their babies are well-rested, not when both mom and baby are physically and emotionally exhausted. Both moms and babies are better able to enjoy being together when baby is alert, energetic, able to focus, and rested. If your baby is always grumpy because he is always tired, your baby is not going to have the ability or desire to connect with you on a deeper level.

Sadly, too often what happens as a result of spending all night fighting, begging, pleading, and even bribing your baby to sleep is that you end up spending the entire next day with two angry people in the room. Brad and I have had so many moms come to us with similar stories about how they were heartbroken to discover they were beginning to resent being up all night rocking and/or nursing their baby. Racked with guilt, moms have told us that they were even beginning to resent the baby they love so very much. Resentfulness, remorse, and guilt are not the stones upon which a healthy relationship is built—certainly not the relationship between a mother and child. Babies are small for a short period of time, and enjoying them without negative emotions or regret is important.

HAVE YOUR CAKE AND EAT IT TOO

On the other side of the room is a little baby who is frustrated long before he is old enough to understand what the word or the feeling means. He wants to express his frustration and so he does, in the only way he knows how: he cries. When your baby cries tears of utter exhaustion and frustration, he is not growing in his attachment to you. Your baby's mind, so young and immature, cannot discern why he feels the way he does. He lacks the cognitive skills to separate and compartmentalize his emotions. The strongest emotion wins.

And then you cry too. You cry because you're feeling guilty. You cry because you're exhausted. You cry realizing that this is not the way things are supposed to be.

Believe me, we understand. We get it. Some people think either we have magical babies that don't cry or that we are somehow crying-prone and it doesn't bother us. We have gone through (and are going through) the same things you are. Our hearts go out to you, and we're here to help.

Part of the problem is that parents wrongly believe that while they are rocking, nursing/feeding and singing their baby to sleep, an attachment is being built between baby and parent. In reality, you're attaching your baby to the thing or the activity that you are providing. Baby is attached to the feeding, not to the mom or dad who is doing the feeding. Your baby is attached to rocking, not to the person rocking him. Your baby is attached to the songs you sing, not to the singer. Get the picture? Your baby is attached to what you provide (remember: "sleep crutches"), not to you.

Before I present you with some research to support the point I just made, there's something I must tell you. It's easy to find research to support your point of view on any topic, on any issue about which you are passionate. It's easy to find people who agree with you. And it's easy to ignore those who don't agree with you. For example: Milk will save your life. Milk will kill you. Just look at the research. You should vaccinate your baby. You shouldn't vaccinate your baby. Just look at the research. You should let your baby cry. You shouldn't let your baby cry. Just look at the research.

RELYING ON RESEARCH

To one extent or another, everybody relies on research. Everybody knows what they have learned. Everybody believes what they've learned. So, here's what Brad and I believe about this subject. However, our belief is based on research *and* experience. We are confident in this information because we have found it to be true, through years of experience—with our own six children, and countless other families who have come to us.

In 2016, a study from Flinders University[1] found that sleep training improved infant sleep and maternal mood and stress levels. The study also showed that no short or long-term, negative effects were evidence as a result of the sleep training. In fact, cortisol levels were actually lower in sleep-trained babies than in babies who were not sleep-trained. These findings, of course, make sense. After all, a consistently fatigued baby (one that is fatigued over long periods of time) is going to experience more stress as a result. Whereas, a well-

1 https://news.flinders.edu.au/blog/2016/05/25/sleep-research-offers-help-for-babies-and-parents/. Accessed on August 13, 2018.

rested baby is naturally going to be more relaxed, peaceful, and happy when he or she is awake.

Flinders University Associate professor and senior lecturer in the School of Psychology, Michael Gradisar, noted:

> While it's well documented that sleep deprivation can cause family distress, including maternal depression, we're hoping these results will add another element to how parents view their responses and how they manage their own and their babies' sleep behaviour.[2]

There are multiple studies to support the findings of the study cited. However, here's what I want you to come away with: If your baby is in a loving and caring environment where his actual needs are being met, a temporary period of training, which includes allowing your baby to cry, will have no lasting, ill-effects on your baby's health.

Allowing your baby to cry will enable you to teach your baby to sleep on his own while, at the same time, building the wonderful attachment between mother and child every parent desires.

I also want you to remember, what happens when you and your baby don't get the rest you both need. By now, we have made you well-aware of the harmful effects of sleep

---

2 Ibid. The full study can be found at: http://pediatrics.aappublications.org/content/pediatrics/early/2016/05/21/peds.2015-1486.full.pdf

deprivation. Again, we want you to weigh in life's balance two things: on the one side, a short period of time (only a couple weeks in most cases) of allowing your baby to cry as part of sleep training, which will result in your baby sleeping on his own and being much happier; or, on the other side, months, maybe even years of restless nights as you continue to provide unhealthy sleep crutches to your child, with the very real possibility your child will cry even more, not less.

On the one side of life's scale, a happy baby that sleeps on his own; on the other side, an unhappy baby that leaves you wondering if you will one day be rocking a teenager to sleep. You know what you want, and so do we. You want your baby to sleep.

> Once your baby has learned the skill of putting himself to sleep, the result will be baby's healthy physical and emotional development.

Now that we've dealt with the elephant in the room, we hope you can see that it's time for the elephant to leave the house. He's overstayed his welcome. Wave goodbye and determine to allow your baby to cry, for a short period of time, to teach him the skill of sleep so that he will cry significantly less.

We know it's uncomfortable to think about—the thought of allowing your baby to cry. It's even more uncomfortable to actually listen to your baby cry. It was uncomfortable for us.

But we are so glad we confronted and evicted the elephant in the room!

As I write this chapter, I am literally days away from the birth of our seventh child. My other children are healthy, happy sleepers. The newest edition to our family will be, too, even if it means a few nights or naps of allowing our baby to cry. And the only elephants in the room will be fluffy and stuffed.

The good news, and our encouragement to you: once your baby has learned the skill of putting himself to sleep, the result will be baby's healthy physical and emotional development, as well as the wonderful experience of healthy attachment between mother and child, for years to come.

By far, the number one characteristic of a sleeping baby is that the baby is happy. Aren't you happy when you get plenty of rest? I know I'm kind of grumpy when I don't get the rest I need. I lack patience with everyone around me. I don't have the energy I need to really give what I need to give to my family (my husband and my children), my home, my church, or my community. I probably wouldn't have to pull your teeth to get you to admit you're a lot like me in this regard.

I hope you are reading the encouraging testimonies from our students, who like you, had babies who wouldn't sleep, and now have happy, well-rested babies. These testimonies will provide you with real life examples, and further motivate you to stick to it—to stay the course and finish the race.

But first, let's get you on the road to a better night's sleep for you and your baby! To do that we need to consider a bit further why your best efforts have failed in the past.

CHAPTER 3
TAKE AWAYS

- A parent's biggest fear is causing damage to their developing baby by letting them cry while learning to sleep.

- Babies will cry whether they are sleep training or not. Putting that crying to good use is what we call "building cry equity".

- There is no research to support that any physical, emotional, or mental damage is done during the sleep training process for babies that live in an otherwise loving and nurturing home.

- By going through a short period of training we may actually reduce overall crying of baby, create better attachments, reduce stress by eliminating sleep deprivation, and bring joy back into the parenting process.

Ashley Garlo   ...

When we began MBCS I was most fearful of the protest. The crying hurt my mommy heart, but I knew that her needs were met and she was learning a lifelong skill. Greta's videos reassured me that the protest was with a purpose. Within 2 days she was putting herself to sleep and within one week sleeping through the night. MBCS transformed our baby and family.

Hillary Carmen
28 mins · 👥

· · ·

As a nanny of 10 years, I thought I knew how to get a baby sleeping. But by 6 weeks, I was desperately sleep deprived and a friend recommended this sleep program. Three days later, we had a scheduled and sleeping baby! There was much less crying than anticipated. Knowing he was safe, fed, and dry and that he was learning an invaluable skill helped make those 3 days worth it.

Stephanie Snodgrass   ...

Let's talk about crying for a minute, this is the hardest part! During the first 3 months, we had hours of crying at night. It was my first and I thought, this is just parenting. What I realized was that feeding on demand and no schedule were the main reasons. This program made being a mom so rewarding, and we are doing it all over again!

Chapter Four

WHY MOST TRAINING FAILS

You may have gotten this far in the book and are still asking the question: "Why has my training failed in the past?" Perhaps you are saying to yourself, "Greta, you don't understand. I've tried *everything*. Nothing works. My child is just different. He doesn't respond to letting him cry. He doesn't respond to sleep training. He doesn't respond to a schedule. So, with all due respect, you simply don't know what you're talking about."

What we are going to do in this chapter is explore the reasons why sleep training for some (maybe you) has failed in the past. It's important to begin by reminding you that you're not alone. Lots of moms have contacted us when they've reached the end of their ropes—when, with exasperation, they have thrown their hands in the air and exclaimed, "Nothing works!"

FLOWERS VS. CHOCOLATE CAKE

As we work our way together through this chapter, I want you to remember this: where we focus our efforts really matters. Are you focusing your efforts, no matter how well-intended, in the right direction or in the wrong direction?

Many of you reading this have, like me, played the "Dating Game." A suitor comes to your door, with flowers in hand—*beautiful* flowers. You look at the fella at your front door, you look at the flowers in his hand, and you think to yourself,

> Are you focusing your efforts, no matter how well-intended, in the right direction or in the wrong direction?

"You know, a big, decadent piece of chocolate cake would have been a better choice. *That* would have wooed me. *That* would have filled my love bucket." Or maybe your husband brings you home a box—a pizza box. His intentions are good. I mean, come on, what woman doesn't like pizza? However, what you really wanted was an ice cream sundae. Both the suitor and husband had good intentions. Their hearts were in the right place. How did they fail? Their efforts were misdirected. They both started with a good idea (making their date or spouse happy) but did not achieve the desired outcome because they did not have all the necessary information (what would *actually* make them happy).

Desperate to find a solution, many parents have dabbled in many different forms of sleep training. They experience the frustration of failure, never experiencing consistent good nights' sleep or productive nap times with their babies. Why? Their good intentions never became a reality because their misdirected efforts missed the mark.

MISGUIDED APPROACHES TO SLEEP TRAINING

Let's take a look at some of the misguided approaches to sleep training. Perhaps you can identify with one of the following "moms."

The Confused Mom
Maybe, before picking up this book, you read many different articles and blogs, by different authors and experts each with their own opinions and approaches. The result: your head is now full of conflicting information. So, you decide to take a little of this and a little of that, and piecemeal together a plan that you think incorporates the best aspects of the many different things you've read. Or, alternatively you recognize that none of the experts seem to agree, so you throw your hands in the air and determine to do nothing. A lot of us have been there, haven't we?

The 'Out-There' Mom
Maybe you've selected a method that is so "out there" that even if you perfectly implemented it, all it can do is fail. Have you ever heard of the "Pick up-Put down" method? This

particular method has mothers picking up and putting down their babies every two minutes when their babies cry. How exactly is a baby supposed to sleep if he or she is being picked up and put down every two minutes?

The 'Bedtime Crammer' Mom

Or, how about this: Are you one of those parents that thinks a good night's sleep begins the 30 minutes before bedtime? During that critical 30 minutes you do everything possible to ready your baby for sleep: warm bath, rice cereal, massage, fresh diaper, sing songs, read books, and then you put your baby down ever-so-quietly while rocking him or her to sleep. The parent does this knowing he or she can never veer from these tasks or the order in which the tasks are performed. Keep in mind, all of these things have to be accomplished while making sure the room is set up with the right lighting and only the right sounds being allowed into baby's ears. The mom or dad who can accomplish all of that in 30 minutes, every single night, would surely be a fearsome thing to behold!

> The goal is a good, full night's sleep, not simply getting your baby to sleep.

Now, your baby may be enabled to relax under the above conditions. You might even get your baby to sleep. But will your baby stay asleep? Usually not. Again, the goal is a good, full night's sleep, not simply getting your baby to sleep.

The 'Diet Hopper' Mom

Maybe you're the "I've tried everything and nothing works" mom, mostly because you haven't stuck with anything long enough. It's kind of like diet hopping, changing from one diet to the next, never sticking with one long enough to see results. Your plan has never been given a reasonable chance for success and one thing is certain: whatever you try halfway won't work. Most moms we speak to on a weekly basis fall into this frustrating category and it is easily fixable, so don't fret! There's hope for you!

The 'House Divided' Mom

Maybe what you've tried in the past to get your baby to sleep and stay asleep hasn't worked because not everyone is on board. Maybe your spouse isn't really on board. Are you getting pressure from extended family members to do things differently—to do what worked for them and their baby? Are there so many competing voices that you're left thinking you can't fully implement any single idea?

The 'Tiny Space' Mom

Are your present living conditions hindering your progress in implementing a plan to get your baby to sleep through the night? Maybe you live in a small, one-bedroom apartment. Or, perhaps you are living with extended family, which is making it difficult for you to follow a regular schedule. These extenuating circumstances (and others) can make it difficult to follow a consistent routine, especially if the adults with whom you live are not all on the same page regarding a good night's sleep for your baby.

You may have misdirected your efforts, or you may be confused about which method to follow, but it all comes down to one thing...

THE #1 REASON

The number one reason people lack consistency in their sleeping baby strategies and fail to accomplish a full night's sleep for their babies is this: they don't have the emotional and mental support they need to navigate through this very challenging time in their lives. As a result, frustrated parents give in, instead of persevering. After all, it's much easier to quit when we don't see immediate results, than to see it through to the desired end.

Your intentions are good, but you abandon the plan, whatever it may be. This is not unlike (dare I say it) New Year's resolutions. You determine that this will be the year to get in shape (even though you've quit a dozen times in years past). Your plan is to go to the gym a minimum of three days a week. Nothing is going to stop you—nothing but you. Life, as it always does, happens. The last Olive Garden commercial or the latest Ben & Jerry's ice cream flavor was more than you can resist. Your work schedule changes. You lose the consistency you developed, and you're disappointed with yourself, once again. The resolution to get your baby to sleep is fraught with similar obstacles. You develop a plan of attack. You determine to see it through, this time, to the very end. Then life happens. You keep trying, though you're quickly beginning to feel defeated. Before you know it, you cast yet another method aside onto the ash heap of "nothing works" and begin to live into a false reality that your baby will never sleep. Tears.

WHAT'S MISSING?

What's missing in the above scenario—the very real scenario that is playing out, night after night, in homes across the world—is support. What's missing in most sleep training efforts, good or bad, is the emotional and mental support of someone who has "been there, done that"—someone who has the experience and knowledge to come alongside the fatigued parents who are at their wits end, and someone who has literally gotten hundreds of babies this age sleeping fast. The result: you work yourself to the point of utter exhaustion with nothing to show for it but a baby who is still crying. Many parents spend more time trying to get their babies to sleep than their babies spend actually sleeping.

THE SECRET

Parents, if you are going to teach your babies the skill of sleeping, you have to focus your efforts in the right place, and in the right direction. We will address mental and emotional support in greater detail, in later chapters. But first, I want to tell you the secret of a good night's sleep.

Drumroll, please!

A good night's sleep begins with…...wait for it…...*a good day*. It really is that simple. Sleep training doesn't begin at night; it begins during the day! It begins by thoughtfully, carefully, and consistently implementing each step in the revolutionary sleep training method Brad and I have developed. And those steps begin during the day, not at night. Training your baby to sleep is a day-long adventure, not merely a last-minute nighttime activity.

By developing consistency in routine and the forming of good habits, you will begin to eliminate some unproductive, common denominators and variables. For example: how do you determine if your baby is waking at night because he or she has a wet diaper, or because he didn't have enough awake time during the day? Is it gas? Reflux? A need to burp? Or is it because baby is actually hungry? Well, if your baby has no consistency in his daytime routine, then you may be grasping at straws to determine what caused your baby to wake in the middle of the night.

> The secret to a good night is a good day.

So, an integral part of training your baby to sleep through the night is first making sure all of your baby's daytime needs are met: feeding, playtime, exercise, naps, etc. Following the process Brad and I have developed will ensure the meeting of your baby's daytime needs, so you will be able to discern the reason your baby is awake at night. You will stop the unproductive reaction of assuming your baby is hungry when your baby either won't go to sleep or wakes up in the middle of the night.

In the next chapter, you will learn how you can apply these truths to your specific situation, and how to start the sleep training process—the one that will *work*—with your baby. So, turn the page!

CHAPTER 4
TAKE AWAYS

- Your sleep training efforts in the past may have failed for several reasons, including: confusion of which method to follow, following a "crazy method", not following any method through to the end, disagreements on which method to follow, or physical limitations.

- The number one reason most people fail in sleep training is actually due to not having the emotional and mental support to follow through, much like your personal trainer at the gym.

- The real secret to that good night that you have been missing is: A GOOD DAY!

Audra Jenkins is with **Forrest Jenkins.** · · ·
47 mins · 👥

From birth to 5.5 weeks old, my husband & I struggled with a very fussy baby; he cried too often & would only sleep in our arms. Then we found **#mybabycansleep**. From Day 1 of training, tears became few and far between! Kaid became happy during awake time & would actually sleep on his own in his crib!😃We are so blessed to have found Brad & Greta!🙏

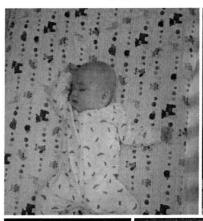 

👍 3   1 Comment

Tessa Loos
1 min · 👥

···

With our baby turning 1, we have done a lot of reflecting on the past year. I am truly amazed to say that he has slept 12+ hours through the night, every night, since he was 10 weeks old. Mybabycansleep.com training was a true blessing and God sent. After all the challenges we experienced with our first born, who didn't sleep through the night until he was nearly 2 years old, I cannot say enough how grateful we are for MBCS! Life changing!

Tommi Teigen Glines   • • •
3 hours ago • 🖼

We can sleep because our baby can sleep! We tried several programs, but nothing seemed to help our youngest learn to sleep on his own. The facebook support group, mentor sessions, flexibility, and structured play suggestions are what made it the absolute best program. Brad and Greta offer biblical wisdom that brought peace and sleep to our home!

👍 Jaclyn Fuller and 4 others   3 Comments

Chapter Five

GOOD NIGHTS START WITH GOOD DAYS

Now that you know the secret to a good night is a good day, how do you get there? A consistent schedule throughout the whole day that stabilizes baby's metabolism is where we need to start, and you're in luck! We'll show you how to get there in this chapter.

WHY IT'S SO HARD TO GET ON A SCHEDULE

There are two primary reasons why parents find it so difficult to get their babies on a schedule. One reason is they don't know how to navigate from where they're at now to where they need to be. The other reason is they simply don't know how to stick to a good schedule once they've found one. They don't know how to consistently manage baby's day.

If you've done any research on baby schedules, you've likely seen a lot of what appear to be good suggestions. On the surface, some might even look like the perfect fix. You've seen them—those perfect schedules: two-hour naps; early, 7:30 pm bedtimes; followed by a wondrous, glorious, 7:00 am wake-up, with no waking up in between. But how in the world do you get your baby to stick to this seemingly *perfect* schedule? Better yet, how do *you* stick to the schedule? If your baby won't sleep for more than 30 minutes at a time and she wants to eat every two hours, how is it possible to get them to take two-hour naps, go four hours between feedings, and then sleep an entire 11-hour night? That seems absolutely impossible, especially to most parents who have never gone through sleep training!

But it's not impossible. In fact, for a four-month-old baby (we work with several hundred four-month-olds alone in our program) it's the norm. It can be the norm for you and your baby, too. We're going to help you get there!

THE ORDER OF EVENTS IN YOUR BABY'S DAY

The very first step in creating a consistent, working schedule for you and your baby is establishing an order of events for your baby's day. This is critically important.

The three key events to your baby's day are eat, play, and sleep—precisely in that order. This cycle will repeat itself throughout the day, three to five times, depending on baby's age. Most parents unintentionally follow a reverse order of events: eat, sleep, play. In order to organize your baby's day and her metabolism, you have to follow the "eat, play, sleep" order of events. Let's look at these events, one-by-one.

Eat

Full feedings are absolutely essential to your baby's sleep training. It's more than simply making sure your baby's tummy is topped-off before bedtime. Rather, it's the *accumulation of sufficient calories throughout the day* that gives your baby the ability to sleep through the night without needing additional feedings.

Work hard to make sure your baby is receiving full feedings during every feeding throughout the day, and this will go a long way toward your baby experiencing good and consistent naps, which leads to great nights' sleeps. This will take effort on your part. You will need to do everything you can to keep your baby awake during feeding to make sure she is getting a full feeding.

> It's the accumulation of sufficient calories throughout the day that gives your baby the ability to sleep through the night.

Play

The second event of your baby's day is playtime. This is the time after the feeding and before naptime. This is the time when your baby expels as much of her energy as possible.

Get creative during this time. Make baby's playtime interactive by stimulating your baby with lots of conversations, or give her some independent playtime as well.

Sleep

The last event in this cycle is sleep. Again, I am referring to naptime during the day. This is most new parents' favorite time because it can be such a productive time. It's a time when your arms are free of baby. The many benefits of this method includes giving attention to your other children if you have them, getting things done around the house, being able to schedule a phone call or event, or even working from home. It's amazing the amount of productivity you can achieve when you get predictable two-hour stretches of time consistently every day.

So, why does this order of events (eat, play, sleep) work so well? To begin with, full feedings result in happy wake times. When your baby's tummy is full your baby is happy. A hungry baby with an unsatisfied appetite is a grumpy baby.

With a full stomach, your baby has more energy, which results in longer and more productive wake times. If your baby expends a sufficient amount of energy she gained from a good feeding, your baby will be tired. Seems obvious, doesn't it? As a result, a tired baby takes good naps.

If your baby is sleeping well during naptime, then she is ready for a great, full feeding when she is awake. Can you see how this cycle builds upon itself? It is an ideal schedule that creates a good day for both parent and baby.

WHY "EAT, SLEEP, PLAY" DOESN'T WORK

With the above in mind, let's talk about why the "eat, sleep, play" cycle (notice the change in order of events) doesn't work.

First of all, when sleep comes after eating the sleep is usually on top of something less than a full feeding. This leads to several problems. First, your baby will likely prematurely awake from naps—one, because she is already hungry again; and two, because she didn't get to burn energy during playtime to prepare her for a good nap.

If your baby is waking early from naps, then you will have shorter times between feedings. This will result in your baby snacking to top off the tank, instead of experiencing a full feeding. As a result of this, baby can't sustain the energy level they need to go three or four hours between feedings. (Don't worry we'll show you exact schedules and times in Chapter Seven.)

Secondly, the "eat, sleep, play" cycle can cause your baby to develop the habit of snacking. If you are nursing and your baby forms a habit of snacking, then she is not getting the rich nutritious hind milk. (The longer baby nurses in a single sitting, the higher the fat content of the milk becomes, which makes full feedings even more important). Snack feedings can also lead to cluster feeding at any time of the day or worse, any time of the night.

Under the "eat, sleep, play" cycle feeding can also become a sleep crutch. Remember talking about sleep crutches in Chapter Two? When feeding comes immediately before sleep, baby begins to associate feeding with sleeping, to the point of not being able to sleep without eating first. As a result, every time baby wakes, she needs the sleep crutch of eating to lull herself back to sleep.

> Snack feedings can also lead to cluster feeding at any time of the day or worse, any time of the night.

Lastly, under the "eat, sleep, play" cycle, babies are likely to be fussier when awake because they are not sleeping through those first signs of hunger. On the more effective "eat, play, sleep" cycle, your baby is able to sleep through those initial tummy grumbles because they went to bed more tired from play time. When they do wake up, they are truly hungry and ready for a full feeding.

Let's summarize, the counter-productive "eat, sleep, play" cycle results in: shorter times of eating, sleeping, and playing; more frequent feedings; less quality feedings; and less predictably in your baby's schedule. It perpetuates a vicious cycle of your baby not being awake enough to take in a full feeding, followed by your baby not being able to get a full nap because they didn't get a full feeding (in addition to the bad sleep crutch this can create), which makes nighttime so hard because they have to eat to get back to sleep. For too many families it is all too familiar.

The "eat, play, sleep" cycle is a much more effective cycle; a cycle that will repeat itself consistently and predictably throughout the day with your guidance. When we discuss schedules in the coming chapters, we will help you determine the age-appropriate "eat, play, and sleep" time intervals that are right for your baby and you.

NAP TRAINING

The second step in achieving a good day for you and your baby is nap training. Now that we've removed the feeding as a sleep crutch, we have to teach your baby how to sleep independently. We also have to learn to connect sleep cycles, which we will talk about in just a bit.

Most people who start sleep training do it at night. Maybe this is you. Frankly, you have to be a superwoman to make it work. It's very difficult. It's best to start sleep training during the day, when you are fresh and alert. It's helpful to begin the work of sleep training during the time of day when normal distractions work to your benefit, helping to keep your mind in a good place.

If you try to start your sleep training at night, you're doing so during the time of day when your family is tired. They are ready to rest, not ready to work. The family is ready to draw the day to a close and get some sleep.

Beginning the sleep training process at night is not only more difficult on parents and siblings, but it's more difficult for your baby. Think about it: Your baby has probably never been put down to sleep alone. On top of that, your baby is being placed in a dark room where she can't see anything. She's never experienced that kind of separation from mom.

> It's best to start sleep training during the day, when you are fresh and alert.

This is why naptime is a great time to start on the first day of your baby's sleep training. Fighting the smaller nap battles first is easier, with a shorter amount of time for sleep. Then both you and baby will have a little experience when approaching the more difficult battle of trying to sleep at night.

Training your baby to sleep at naptime allows your baby to experience a wonderful, full feeding with mom or dad when she wakes up and gets out of bed during the day. A feeding after naptime allows for the parent and baby to bond well, without the stress of trying to force a baby back to sleep while trying to eliminate a feeding (or multiple feedings) at night.

Nap training your baby first inevitably makes training to sleep at night easier. 85-90% of our parents who begin their sleep training during the day very quickly have their babies sleeping at night—sometimes as soon as the night following the first day of training! It's not uncommon for our parents' babies to experience a full night's sleep within one to three nights of beginning the daytime training cycle. This is why naptime training is critically important to our parents' success.

ELEMENTS OF TRAINING YOUR BABY TO SELF-SOOTHE

There are two elements of training your baby to self-soothe. First, baby has to learn how to get to sleep initially. If you don't train your baby to self-soothe and instead use outside stimuli and crutches to get her to sleep, when she awakes from a sleep cycle she will expect/need that same stimulus to get back to sleep.

Second, baby must learn how to connect sleep cycles. Getting to sleep is one thing; staying asleep or falling back to sleep is another thing altogether.

STEP ONE: INITIALLY FALLING ASLEEP

When it is naptime, lay your baby down fully awake. Depending on your baby's age, this may or may not include a swaddle. We recommend swaddling babies from birth until two to four months, when their startle reflex starts to diminish. The next time your baby comes out of bed is when naptime is scheduled to be over, and not before that time (more about this when we talk about connecting sleep cycles). Then, you commence with your baby's scheduled feeding.

Non-Drowsy

It's important I explain, here, what it means to lay your baby down *fully awake*. Maybe you've heard it said that the key to getting your baby down for a nap is making them drowsy. The opposite is actually true. When you put your baby in the crib or bassinet, you do not want to spend any time making them drowsy, or they will need to be drowsy to fall back asleep as well. Whatever state in which baby is put down, will be the state in which baby learns to go back to sleep.

Think about when your baby awakes from that first sleep cycle. Is she going to be drowsy? Probably not. That's why you shouldn't put your baby to bed in a drowsy state. When it's time for nap, your baby might be visibly tired, rubbing her eyes, or showing some other signs of fatigue. Or, your baby might not be showing any signs of fatigue at all. In any case, they key is not putting your baby to bed drowsy.

Will your baby cry if you do this? Probably. Brad and I like to refer to this kind of crying as "protest crying." Here's how to address your baby's protest crying.

THREE WAYS TO HANDLE PROTEST CRYING

There are three different methods for handling your baby's

protest crying at naptime. The differences between them are geared more towards the preference of mom, not necessarily the effectiveness of the methods. After working with over 1,000 families inside our Sleep Accelerator Course, we've found one of these seems to work faster for both mom and baby, but let's go through all three as they will each get the desired end result.

The Extinction Method

The first method is known as "The Extinction Method." This method is simply putting your baby down at naptime and not picking up your baby again until naptime is complete. So, if your baby's scheduled naptime is 9:00 am to 11:00 am, you put your baby down and say, "I love you, and I'll see you when naptime is over." The first day, baby may accomplish getting to sleep but she may only sleep for one cycle (30-45 min). Leaving her is critical for her to learn to connect to another, and yet another sleep cycle (more on this later).

The Gradual Extinction Method

The second method is known as "The Gradual Extinction Method." In this method, you make regular checks of your baby, at regular intervals, while baby is crying. If you choose to go with this method, we recommend you do not pick up your baby unless there is an immediate need, such as a brief burping, cleaning up a wet burp, or a diaper change. Otherwise, if you pick up your baby and then put her back down, she could get angry because an expectation of feeding or comfort was not met.

With this method, it's up to you to decide at what intervals you want to make your checks of the baby. Normal intervals range from 10-15 minutes. If your baby starts to cry after putting her down, set a timer for ten minutes. If after ten minutes your baby is still in a full-on cry, go in, put your hand on your baby's tummy or back (without rubbing); tell her that she is okay, and then walk back out of the room. Some parents believe doing this gives baby the reassurance that she is not alone. These interval checks are then repeated each time the baby cries.

Now, with this method, if your baby is showing signs of slowing down or she is only crying intermittently, don't go in to check on the baby. These are signs that your baby is starting to put herself to sleep.

Let's review this method.

I put my baby down and she is crying. I set my timer for ten minutes. She's still in a full-on cry after ten minutes. I go into the room, put my hand on my baby's tummy or back, without patting or rubbing. I give her some reassurance, and then I walk out of the room. If she is still crying, I reset my timer for ten minutes. If my baby is still in a full-on cry after another ten minutes, I repeat the process.

Having left the room for a second time, I begin to hear my

baby show signs of slowing down. If my baby is not in a full-on cry after another ten minutes, I leave my baby alone to put herself to sleep. And I rejoice at the progress made!

Let's say my baby were to wake up after 30 minutes, once again full-on crying. I set my timer for ten minutes and repeat the process. I continue to repeat the process until baby shows signs of putting herself to sleep or until naptime is over, whichever comes first.

The Fading Method

The third method is called "The Fading Method." Success with this method takes longer to achieve than the other two methods. However, this method can be beneficial to parents who are uncomfortable leaving their babies to cry alone, in their cribs. It does not necessarily benefit baby (and may make it more challenging for baby to sleep), but it can be helpful for a parent's peace of mind.

In this method, you sit in a chair next to your baby's bed or crib and, without making eye or physical contact, wait for your baby to fall asleep. Once you baby falls asleep, you leave the room. Every few days (the amount of time can vary, based on your baby's sleep progress) you gradually move your chair away from the baby's bed or crib until you are finally out of the room. If your baby awakes, you simply go back into the room and sit down wherever you were sitting before your baby fell asleep.

Again, this method takes the longest of the three, which, in and of itself, can make it the most difficult for parents. One reason for the difficulty is sitting next to your baby while your baby is crying, without doing anything to comfort your baby.

All three of these methods are proven to work. It's really up to you as to which method you choose to employ, based on your personality and home-life circumstances.

The "Extinction Method" is by far the fastest of the three methods for nap training. Needless to say, this is most beneficial for both parents and babies because you are "ripping off the Band-Aid," as we like to say. You are putting your baby in a certain set of circumstances. Your baby quickly realizes those circumstances aren't going to change because she is crying. With this method, your baby learns very quickly that this is the "new norm."

STEP TWO: CONNECTING REM CYCLES

The second step in training is teaching baby to connect cycles of Rapid Eye Movement (REM) sleep. You will use one of the methods stated above to accomplish this, as we want to teach baby the skill of going back to sleep on her own and bridge her REM sleep cycle. Let me explain...

Dolphins and REM Cycles

When you think about sleep, I want you to think about dolphins. That's right, dolphins. Picture, if you will, dolphins diving in and out of the water. A dolphin's deep dive represents your baby's deep sleep pattern. The dolphin rising again to the surface represents your baby's light sleep. Everyone experiences deep sleep and light sleep cycles. We experience them, and so does your baby. These deep and light sleep cycles go by other names: REM sleep and non-REM sleep; or active sleep and passive sleep.

Most babies can accomplish the initial, deep, non-REM sleep on their own. You've seen this. You will rock your baby and next thing you know your baby is passed-out on your lap or shoulder. You can flop her around. It seems that if an earthquake struck it wouldn't phase her a bit. *Nothing*, so it seems, is going to wake your baby from that deep sleep.

However, after about 30-45 minutes, after that initial deep sleep cycle, your baby comes up to her lighter sleep cycle and she wakes up. If you've placed sleep crutches in your baby's life, this is when your baby will crave them. She will be looking for her crutch to get back to sleep, and likely won't go back to sleep without it.

Just as a dolphin dives deep and rises to the water's surface, every human being experiences these sleep cycles. A key to getting your baby to stay asleep is teaching her to connect these cycles together, without the help of any outside association (crutch).

It's very important I note something, at this point. No one

sleeps completely through the night. Everyone wakes during the night, to one extent or another. You might wake up, roll over, and quickly go back to sleep. You might wake up, visit the bathroom, and go back to sleep. If a person has a medical condition like sleep apnea, he or she may awake several times every hour! You are likely so good at putting yourself back to sleep that you often don't remember waking during the night.

Again, babies who have been conditioned to need a sleep crutch won't go back to sleep until they get that crutch. So, how do you teach your baby to connect her sleep cycles, without the need for or use of crutches? How do you train your baby to self-soothe back to sleep?

> You are likely so good at putting yourself back to sleep that you often don't remember waking in the night.

Naptime Is Naptime

The first step in teaching your baby to connect her sleep cycles is giving her the chance to learn on her own. Most parents rush to their baby way too quickly, when their baby first wakes up.

In our program, I always like to say, "Naptime is naptime." What do I mean by that? It means that no matter what, the scheduled naptime is the time in which the baby is in her crib for nap. Again, in the coming chapters, you will find the age-appropriate schedule for your baby. You may find you need to tweak the schedule a bit since our babies are not robots—they are individuals with individual needs.

CONSISTENCY

Regardless of what method you choose, the key to success is consistency. Your baby's body must be guided into a rhythm. Your baby must be given the opportunity to learn to connect these sleep cycles. If your form of consistency is to prematurely get your baby up during naptime, then you are teaching your baby that she doesn't have to learn to put herself back to sleep.

If your baby's nap and feeding times are different every day, your baby will not come to expect what's next. As human beings, we are creatures of habit. This means your baby is also a creature of habit, craving routine and structure. If you provide your baby with the proper structure during the day, your baby will come to expect the consistency such structure provides. Again, consistency is the key to any training, especially baby sleep training.

> *Regardless of what method you choose, the key to success is consistency.*

Naptime on day one is when your baby should begin learning to connect her sleep cycles. It may be hard work for the first few days, but that's okay! Naptimes could take two to four weeks of consistent training to go smoothly from start to finish.

Now that I've told you about your first day of training, let's take a look at your baby's first night of training.

CHAPTER 5
TAKE AWAYS

- The first step in training is getting your baby on a consistent EPS (eat, play, sleep) schedule. This allows for full feedings, great awake time, and the elimination of sleep crutches.

- The second step to having a great night is naptime training.

- There are two elements to sleep training: teaching baby to fall asleep initially, and helping baby to learn to connect REM cycles.

- To teach baby to put herself to sleep, put her down fully-awake, not drowsy!

- There are three main methods to sleep training, all of which will ultimately accomplish the goal of sleep: the Extinction Method, the Gradual Extinction Method, and the Fading Method.

- The second half to nap training is teaching baby to connect REM cycles. Naptime is naptime. Let baby learn to connect REM cycles by giving her the opportunity to put herself back to sleep.

- In all of our training, consistency is key!

Amber Wood

16 minutes ago · 🖼

···

MBCS taught us how to teach our kids to nap. With twins, napping was necessary in those first months to get anything done around the house. Now napping toddlers equal happy toddlers, which allows us to take them on fun adventures without meltdowns.

👍 Like   💬 Comment

Katie Sturm   · · ·

· 1 minute ago · 🖼

MBCS has been incredible for our family, first for our 2nd child and now for our newborn, Elsa! Having her on an EPS has given our family more predictability and really awesome nights. At 3 weeks old she is doing 4 hour stretches between feedings at night!

♡ 1

Melissa Weber is with **Ryan Weber Ifbb Pro**.

48 mins · 🌐

How do we make time for the gym and competitions with a little one? We used the My Baby Can Sleep Program. It gave us everything we needed to support us having a successful EPS (eat, play, sleep) schedule and routine. Logan learned to put himself to sleep and was sleeping 10 hours/night by 8 weeks. By the time I went back to the gym we had a routine that fit our lifestyle and Logan's needs.

Chapter Six

THE (NOT SO) DREADED NIGHT TRAINING

We've now discussed those good days—setting up your baby on a great daytime routine. We've discussed nap training, full feedings, and breaking those bad habits and associations that your baby might build into sleep crutches. We've discussed sleep cycles and how to bridge them together. Now, it's time for us to discuss the dreaded night training. Don't be fearful or discouraged. As you will soon see, it's not as difficult as you might think.

WHAT IS SLEEPING THROUGH THE NIGHT?

Before we talk about how to train your baby to sleep through the night, we have to define what that means. We define *sleeping through the night* as seven to eight hours of sleep. This may include brief wakings, however, no intervention is necessary and baby can resume sleeping without help or a feeding.

Typically, you should not expect newborns (babies under eight weeks gestational age) to sleep as long as, say, a six-month-old. Newborns will likely need one to two nighttime feedings, in addition to the dream feed (explained later in this chapter). So keep this in mind as you read this section. But even in those newborn weeks, we aim to get the most age appropriate sleep for baby.

BEDTIME

Let's start with bedtime. You will see in our sample schedules that we recommend putting baby down for bed between 7:00 and 8:00 pm. Most moms and dads we talk to around the world insist on having a bedtime routine. While the bedtime routines for every family are different, there are some similarities. Common aspects of bedtime routines include: bath, lotion, reading books, singing songs, hugs and kisses, and prayers. Then baby might be rocked a bit and put into his crib.

What I just described is not so much a routine, but rather a list of habits. So, what should bedtime really look like? First, let me affirm that there's nothing wrong with baths, lotion, songs, books, etc. We want to give you the freedom to do those things or not do those things. You can make your bedtime routine (or habits) as extensive or as brief as you like. However, you do not have to follow a specific process to get your baby to sleep through the night.

Remember: it's not the 30 or 60 minutes before bedtime that gets your baby sleeping through the night. Your baby's night should not be dependent on the series of things you do before you put them down in their crib. So, what does a good bedtime routine look like? Here it is—Are you ready?

Do whatever you like!

A good bedtime routine usually does include a feeding. But remember, don't allow feeding to become a sleep crutch by feeding your baby to sleep. After the feeding, you want to make sure to relieve your baby of any trapped gas, especially if he is younger. Then you are going to put your baby down *fully awake*. And remember; don't rock your baby to the point of making your baby drowsy.

> It's not the 30 or 60 minutes before bedtime that gets your baby sleeping through the night.

Lay your baby down, tell him that you love him, and say goodnight. Will he protest? Probably. However, most of our parents find that bedtime goes smoother than naptime training. The length of your baby's protests will likely be shorter at bedtime than at naptime.

If it does take your baby some time to fall asleep, don't worry. Your baby needs to accomplish sleep on his own. When your baby protests, don't go in the room right away to soothe him.

You need to give your baby a good period of time before going into the room to intervene.

If for some reason your baby protests for more than 60-90 minutes after being put down, then you're going to go into your baby's room and offer the dream feed early. I'll explain more about this in a moment. Obviously, your baby won't be dreaming if he's protesting, but that's okay. After you feed your baby, you will place him back in his bed and let him go to sleep on his own. With a full tummy after his workout, baby will likely drift off without much of a fight.

DREAM FEEDING

During the training process, Brad and I ask parents to implement what's called a "dream feed." We use this term loosely during the training process. Simply put, a dream feed is a feeding that takes place around 10:00 pm or sometime shortly before you go to sleep. Since baby is put to bed around 7:00 pm, typically he will be sleeping when you go in to feed him— hence the name *dream feed*. This feeding typically isn't necessary after three to four months of age. But it can be helpful in the training process.

Why do we recommend this extra feeding? Is it really necessary? Here's why we suggest implementing this special feeding.

If your baby is in the habit of nighttime feedings, a nice full feeding before you go to bed serves to give you some peace of mind. If your baby awakes later in the night, it helps to know he had a full feeding not that long ago. For example, if you fed your baby at 10:00 pm, and your baby awakes at midnight, then you can have relative confidence that your baby does not need to eat.

If your baby has a good daytime routine, then you know your baby has been well-fed throughout the day and had ample time to play. So if your baby wakes up a couple hours after the dream feed, you can allow your baby to work himself back to sleep without the stress of wondering if your baby is hungry.

> If your baby has a good daytime routine, then you know your baby has been well-fed and had ample time to play.

You also want to give your baby the right stretch of sleep. Depending on your baby's age, he may not be able to sleep a full 12 hours between two feedings. It's easier to set your sights on an eight- to nine-hour stretch of sleep. Therefore, if you feed your baby around 10:00 pm, or shortly before you go to bed, you can get your baby to stretch his sleep to the time he should be awaking for his next, regular feeding, for example, at 7:00 am. Conversely, if baby can only accomplish a nine-hour stretch of sleep and his last feeding is at 7:00 pm, he will be waking at 4:00 am to be fed and put back to bed. It's up to you, but my preference is to feed my little one before I go to bed, as opposed to getting a 4:00 am wake-up call!

Once your baby has accomplished a 10:00-7:00 or 11:00-7:00 stretch of sleep, then you can start weaning your baby off of the dream feed. To do this, simply move the dream feed earlier by 30 minute increments every few nights. For example, if your baby typically dream feeds at 10:30 pm, and is consistently sleeping from the end of the dream feed until morning wake up time, move your dream feed to 10:00 pm. After a few nights of baby sleeping from 10:00 pm until morning wake up, move your dream feed another 30 minutes earlier to 9:30 pm. Eventually, your dream feed time will meet up with (or come close enough to) your evening feeding time, making it easy to drop completely.

If your baby is sleeping at the time of the dream feed, you can pick your baby up and nurse or give him a bottle. Or, you can give your baby a bottle as he lies in his crib. If your baby is very young, then you may have to wake your baby to give this feeding. With newborns, you will likely have to wake your baby and give him a diaper change along with the dream feed. Don't worry about waking your baby. He will likely fall right back to sleep, with little or no protest, after his dream feed.

Regarding diaper changes: I like to do diaper changes at this time because with babies, whenever you put liquid in, it means liquid pushes out. I don't want my baby to wake during the "wee" hours of the night (pun intended) because he has soaked through his diaper. An uncomfortable baby is going to have a much harder time falling and staying asleep.

After the feeding, give your baby a good burping, and lay him back down to fall asleep on his own. Your baby has a full belly, a clean diaper, a dark room, and will likely fall right back to sleep. Besides beating the timer, which we'll explain in a minute, one of the few reasons you should return to your baby's room after the dream feed is to either burp your baby or if you know your baby needs a change of diaper.

WHAT IF BABY WAKES IN THE MIDDLE OF THE NIGHT?

Let's say you follow the proper steps when putting your baby down. You provide your baby with a timely dream feed, burp and diaper change. Your baby falls back to sleep on his own, but then he awakes in the middle of the night. What should you do?

The timer is your friend.

Each time your baby awakes from sleeping, you will utilize your timer. You can use your phone or watch, or whatever timer you have on hand. Set your timer for 45 minutes. For newborns (up to eight weeks old), we recommend a shorter period of time, anywhere from five to 30 minutes. For babies two months and older, we recommend setting your timer for the full 45 minutes.

Keep your timer running for as long as your baby is crying. If at any point your baby settles down for a few minutes or returns to sleep, shut off your timer. If your baby awakes again, reset your timer for another full 45 minutes. For example: let's say your baby wakes at 2:00 am. You will set your timer for 45 minutes. If your baby starts to settle at 2:30 am, turn the timer off. If your baby awakes five minutes later, reset your time for 45 minutes. When your baby settles, turn your timer off.

Note: you don't have to sleep with your baby monitor next to your ear, with the volume on full blast. We want to make this process as painless as possible. And let me tell you, a loud baby monitor can make the process very, very uncomfortable. The discomfort isn't so much your baby crying, but rather the sometimes ear-piercing frequency and tone with which most baby monitors operate. In most homes, if bedroom doors are kept open, your baby can be heard just fine, without a monitor.

If during the process, your timer goes the full 45 minutes and your baby is still crying, you have a couple of options. If you normally offer your baby a feeding in the middle of the night, then you should do just that. Feed, burp, or change a diaper as you normally would, and then simply lay your baby back down. If you typically go in to give your baby a rocking, instead go in and give your baby a brief comforting. It is best if you can avoid picking your baby up. You don't want to give your baby a false sense of hope that you are going to take him out of his room with you. Simply rub your baby's belly or back, gently reassure and soothe your baby, and then leave the room. Let baby continue to work himself back to sleep and set your timer for another 45 minutes. If baby is still crying at the end of another timer, go in to comfort again. Repeat as necessary until baby puts himself back to sleep.

You will repeat the above process every time your baby awakes until it's time to get your baby up to start the day.

IMPORTANT SIDE NOTE

It's extremely important to start your baby's day on or about the same time, every day. Work to get within 30 minutes of your designated daytime start time. If you've determined that 7:00 am is when your baby will start his day, then shoot for getting your baby up no earlier than 6:30 am. A consistent start time is critical in setting your baby's metabolism. As humans we are creatures of habit. Your baby will be, too. So, establishing a consistent daily start time will help your baby establish good sleeping and waking habits.

OUR PARENTS REPORT

Most of our clients report that their babies do wake on the first night of training, but they typically don't outlast the timer. Again, the reason for our high rate of success is because our clients are doing well in training during the day, which makes training during the night that much easier.

Babies might have short periods of being awake during the night, but again our parents report their babies fall back to sleep relatively quickly. More often than not, intervention is not necessary, even on the first night of training.

> More often than not, intervention is not necessary, even on the first night of training.

Even our parents who report a few nighttime feedings most of them tell us that by the third night of training they experience little or no nighttime protests from their babies. Wouldn't that be great if it happened with your baby, too? It can! It will!

I hope you are getting excited to start the process.

Remember. Nap training does take more time than night training. It can take several weeks to work through the daytime training process, but nighttime training usually happens fairly quickly—usually within a few nights. So, be encouraged!

WHEN BABY BEATS THE TIMER

Now, if you find yourself after a few nights of setting your timer that your baby is still consistently waking and outlasting the 45 minute timer, it could be that your baby has figured out how to beat the timer. Babies are smart! This happens with about 10% of the babies we help train. If you find yourself as one of these rare cases, then you might need to increase the amount of time on your timer. Also, make sure the other elements of your baby's day are on track. Make sure your baby is consuming enough calories. Make sure your baby is getting enough awake time during the day. And be ever mindful of your consistency. Don't increase your nighttime timer until you have evaluated your daytime routine to make sure it's in order. Lastly, don't get discouraged if your baby takes a week or longer to sleep through the night. He will get there!

WHERE SHOULD BABY SLEEP?

Now is a good time to discuss *where* babies should sleep. This can be a controversial issue for some parents because the American Academy of Pediatrics (AAP) and the Centers for Disease Control (CDC) recommend having a baby in his parents' room for the first year of his life, in an effort to prevent Sudden Infant Death Syndrome (SIDS). I want to present both sides of this issue so that you, the parent, can make an informed decision that is best for your family.

We work with many families whose babies have their own rooms at a very early age, and this works well for those families. However, I want to present you with a few pros and cons for having your baby sleep in your bedroom. First, the cons.

Most babies, when they wake in the middle of the night, will cry in protest. No matter the baby's age, the baby will know that mom and/or dad is in the same room. This poses a couple of problems. First, the presence of another person in the room can be very stimulating for the baby. Knowing you are in the room might lead to your baby wanting to play instead of sleep. If you are a nursing mom, baby can even smell your milk and think it is time to eat. Secondly, being in the room with your baby can make it challenging for you to outlast your baby's protest, in the middle of the night. Who wants to (or can) sleep next to their babies when he is crying? Thirdly, with you in the room your baby will likely learn precisely how much protest is necessary to achieve his desired goal—your undivided attention. Again, babies are smart. As a result of having your baby in your bedroom, the chances of your baby putting themselves back to sleep greatly diminishes, especially in the early morning hours.

Some parents, out of frustration and exhaustion, not wanting to repeatedly get out of bed to address their baby's (real or perceived) needs, end up having their baby sleep in bed with them. This poses its own problems, not the least of which putting your baby's safety at risk. Many babies have died as a result of being inadvertently smothered by a parent or bedding.

Having looked at the cons of having your baby in the same room with you at night, let's look at a couple pros. First (and this probably goes without saying), you are right there and ready to immediately respond to your baby's needs. Second: while there is certainly no guarantee, having your baby in such close proximity may possibly prevent the tragedy of SIDS.

THE CHOICE IS YOURS

Every family is unique. You need to decide whether you want your baby and family to experience long, consistent sleep at night, or the peace of mind that comes with having your baby near you all night long. Take your time in making this decision. Make sure to weigh the pros and cons I've identified, as well as any other factors specific to your family.

You can also consider finding middle ground. If you don't want your baby down the hall, in another room, but you don't want your baby next to your bed or in bed with you, consider having your baby sleep in an area somewhere in between. For example: if you have a master bedroom with your own bathroom, you might consider putting a pack-and-play in a safe area of the bathroom. This way your baby is closer to you, but not too close. Or, if you have a big walk-in closet with plenty of space—having eliminated potential dangers of something falling off a shelf, or clothes surrounding your baby too closely—you might consider this as an option.

SAFE SLEEP IN BABY'S ROOM

If you do decide to allow your baby to sleep in his own room, let's talk about how to do that in the safest way possible, according to the AAP guidelines.

When you place your baby in a crib, at least for the first year of his life, you want to make sure there is nothing else in the crib. No bumpers; no blankets; no stuffed animals or toys of any kind. You don't want anything in the crib that could somehow obstruct your baby's breathing and cause suffocation. Additionally, a safe sleep for your baby means using tight-fitting sheets in the crib, and nothing else. If you are concerned about your baby getting cold at night, then you can use a safe swaddle, sleep sack, or warm pajamas. Taking these simple precautions may protect your baby from SIDS or suffocation.

Okay. Now that you know how to handle your baby's nighttime wakings, let's work together to identify the best schedule for you and your baby.

CHAPTER 6
TAKE AWAYS

- Sleeping through the night is defined as sleeping 7-8 hours without intervention.

- A bedtime routine can be a simple or complex as you desire, and does not need to be exactly the same from one night to the next.

- Implement a dream feed for younger infants or older babies during the training process for a few extra calories, peace of mind, and to help establish the right stretch of sleep.

- To implement the dream feed, wake baby and feed before you go to bed. As baby is able to make the entire stretch to morning without a feeding, move the feeding earlier by 30 minute increments every few nights.

- When baby wakes in the middle of the night, set your timer for 45 minutes. If he goes back to sleep or settles in that time, turn your timer off. If baby wakes a few minutes later, reset your timer for 45 minutes. If he does not go back to sleep within that time, offer a feeding or a brief comforting. Repeat each time he wakes.

- Make safe sleep decisions for your baby, whether he is in your room or in his own room.

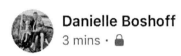

Danielle Boshoff
3 mins · 🔒

···

Tahlia was up 10-12 x a night. I dropped her sleep crutches and started the 45 min timer. I felt comfortable knowing I could check on her after the 45 minutes. But I never had to , she fell asleep before the time was up . She was on a normal nap routine within the first 2- 3 days, and slept all night straight on the third night . My baby can sleep saved us .

👍 Like   💬 Comment

Erica Aldredge Spiva

6 hrs · 👥   · · ·

I can't wait to take these two on another adventure. **#MBCS** saved our sanity. After 8 months 'trying everything,' the twins slept through the night on night #2, after learning to take long consistently timed naps at the SAME TIME! At night the 45 min timer gave me a boundary I was comfortable with, though they never beat it! 🙌😴 ♥️👨‍👩‍👧

👍❤️ Kellie Walker and 31 others   4 Comments

Julie Lanfair
27 mins · 👥 · · ·

I was at wits end with sleepless nights when my daughter was 5 months old. Thankfully, around that same time, I ran across an ad for **#mybabycansleep** and looked into it. Brad and Greta helped save my sanity! After less than a week Skyler was sleeping through the night and after 3-4 weeks she was napping on schedule. She was a much happier baby and I was a MUCH more enjoyable mama. She is an even more enjoyable 22 month old now with the program's toddler training too! Brad and Greta know what they are talking about and it works!

👍 Like   💬 Comment

Chapter Seven

BABY'S FIRST YEAR AND BEYOND

In the pages of this chapter, you will find typical schedules for each age group, through a baby's first year of life, and a little beyond. The key word here is "typical." Every baby is different. Babies are not robots. They are not wind-up toys. They are unique individuals.

With that in mind, I want you to view the schedules provided with the understanding that you have the flexibility to adjust any of the schedules, based on your baby's specific needs. You may determine you need to shift the schedule times either forward or backward to meet your family's needs. For example: each of our sample schedules start at 7:00 am, but your family gets up and going at 6:00 am. Simply shift the entire schedule (i.e. naps, feeds, and bedtime) up one hour.

KEYS TO STARTING YOUR SCHEDULE

Here are a few important considerations before starting your baby's schedule:

1. Calculate your baby's awake time. Awake time starts when you get your baby up from her nap and you begin her feeding. With young infants, the whole awake time, or the majority of it, might be the feeding. Note: awake time includes both feeding and playtime.

2. Determine the ideal "sweet spot." In the early days of your baby's life, awake time lengths are critically important and finding a "sweet spot" for your baby's awake time is likewise extremely important. The sweet spot is the perfect amount of awake time where baby will drift off to sleep with little to no protest and sleep an entire nap. If your baby's naps are consistently not going well with the amount of awake time you've chosen for your baby, change it by five or ten minutes to see if you can find that ever-important "sweet spot."

3. Account for stomach size and calories. The older your baby gets the easier sleep training will likely become. For a newborn baby, we consider her stomach's size and ability to hold enough calories throughout the day. This is important in determining whether or not a baby can sleep through the night. For older infants, this is less a concern, as long as you focus on full feedings.

4. It's not too late to train your toddler. Many parents of toddlers wrongly believe they've missed the window

of opportunity to train their babies. This simply isn't the case. Children two years old (and even older) can be trained to sleep through the night. A good day for a toddler will include working not only on sleeping during naptime, but also obedience to authority figures. Obedience training will make a huge difference at bedtime, too.

NOTE ON CAT NAPS

While you browse the schedules below you may notice a nap at the end of the day referred to as the "cat nap." This is my favorite nap for a few reasons. This is the time of day we can really let baby be in control of nap time. Watch carefully for her sleepy cues, as she may not have the typical amount of awake time before this nap. If she has had three successful naps, she may have a little extra energy to burn in the evening, which may mean a little more awake time before she is ready for another nap. The cat nap can range in length from 30 minutes to a full two hours. A newborn will probably take a longer cat nap than a five-month-old, for example. Just make sure she has appropriate awake time and stimulation before putting her to bed for the night, which means, bedtime may need a slight adjustment from the written schedule if baby has taken a longer cat nap.

Another reason this is my favorite nap is that it is a "sleep anywhere" nap. Many sleep-trained babies are fabulous sleepers...when they are in their own crib in their own room.

But we all know that life happens and we can't be home for every single nap and bedtime every single day. The cat nap gives us an opportunity to train baby to sleep in other places, in other circumstances with lights, noise, and movement. So take this opportunity to grab your baby carrier and give baby a nap while you are doing some vacuuming. Or pull out the portable crib to test out a nap in a new room. Get some exercise and go for a walk while baby sleeps in the stroller. Or maybe you just snuggle up on the couch with your little bundle and enjoy the snuggles before those days slip away.

Sleep training doesn't have to confine us to our homes 24/7. Flexibility and freedom can be a part of our normal routine as well.

Now let's take a look at schedules.

NEWBORN DAYS

You can start your newborn's daytime schedule with the 2.5- or 3-hour schedule. This will be determined by your baby's feeding needs and your baby's ability to stay awake. If you decide to begin with the 2.5-hour schedule, move up to the next schedule when your baby is ready for more awake time or extended time between feedings.

Note, naptimes vary depending on baby's needs and ability to stay awake. For example, you will see in the following schedule that the first nap is scheduled for 7:45/8:00 am.

This means baby can be put down for a nap anytime between 7:45 and 8:00 am. Also, our 0-8 weeks schedules include two middle-of-the-night feedings in which you will wake baby to feed. When you know baby is gaining weight well and your milk supply is well-established (for nursing moms) you may let baby wake up naturally for a feeding. This typically occurs at one to two weeks of age. After this time, you can let baby wake on her own to eat.

When she wakes, give her a few minutes to either fully wake up, or possibly work herself back to sleep. If she is still awake after a few minutes, offer a feeding, doing your best to keep baby awake and actively eating. You will notice that baby will gradually start to extend the time between feedings. Most babies can sleep seven to eight hours between feedings by eight weeks of age!

Sample Schedule 0-8 Weeks
(2.5-hour cycle)

7:00 am – First morning feeding
7:45/8:00 am – Nap
9:30 am – Mid-morning feeding
10:15/10:30 am – Nap
12:00 pm – Afternoon feeding
12:45/1:00 pm – Nap
2:30 pm – Mid-afternoon feeding
3:15/3:30 pm – Nap
5:00 pm – Late afternoon feeding

6:00 pm – Cat nap (30-45 min)

7:30 pm – Evening feeding and bed

10:30 pm – Dream feed and back to bed

1:00 am – Scheduled feeding for baby who is 1-2 weeks old; feed and back to bed

4:00 am – Scheduled feeding for baby who is 1-2 weeks old; feed and back to bed

After 1-2 weeks of age you will not wake baby for feeding, you will wait for baby to wake you.

Sample Schedule 0-8 Weeks

(3-hour cycle)

7:00 am – First morning feeding

7:50/8:10 am – Nap

10:00 am – Mid-morning feeding

10:50/11:00 am – Nap

1:00 pm – Afternoon feeding

1:50/2:10 pm – Nap

4:00 pm – Late afternoon feeding

5:10 pm – Cat nap (30-45 min, possibly longer if baby likes)

7:00 pm – Evening feeding and bed

10:00 pm – Dream feed and back to bed

1:00 am – Scheduled feeding for baby who is 1-2 weeks old; feed and back to bed

4:00 am – Scheduled feeding for baby who is 1-2 weeks old; feed and back to bed

After 1-2 weeks of age you will not wake baby for feeding, you will wait for baby to wake you.

8-16 WEEKS: SCHEDULE AND TRANSITIONS

When your baby reaches 8-16 weeks of age, she is ready for more awake time, as well as more time between feedings. You do not need to make the transition to these longer cycles right at eight weeks of age. Wait until you are sure your baby is ready for this transition. Some babies like to move past a 3-hour cycle at eight weeks. Other babies don't accomplish this until 14-16 weeks old. You know your baby best. Make the transition when you believe your baby is ready.

Note: typical awake times may vary by 15-30 minutes.

By 12-14 weeks age, many babies are ready to drop the late evening dream feed. You can choose to keep the dream feed going as long as you deem necessary to get your baby a few more calories throughout the day. **If you do decide to drop the dream feed, and you are nursing, a pumping session in place of the feeding is necessary to keep your supply from diminishing.**

Sample Schedule 8-16 Weeks
(3.5-hour cycle)

7:00 am – Feeding
8:30 am – Nap
10:30 am – Feeding
12:00 pm – Nap
2:00 pm – Feeding
3:30 pm – Nap

5:30 pm – Feeding

7:00 pm – Bedtime

10:00 pm – Optional dream feed

Sample Schedule 8-16 Weeks

(Modified 3.5-hour cycle)

7:00 am – Feeding

8:30 am – Nap

10:30 am – Feeding

12:00 pm – Nap

2:00 pm – Feeding

3:30 pm – Nap

5:00 pm – Feeding

6:30 pm – Cat nap (30-45 min)

8:00 pm – Feeding and bed

10:30 pm – Dream feed

Sample Schedule 8-16 Weeks

(4-hour cycle)

7:00 am – Feeding

8:30/8:45 am – Nap

11:00 am – Feeding

12:30/1:00 pm – Nap (let baby sleep as long as they like)

3:00 pm (or upon waking after 3:00) – Feeding

5:00 pm – Cat nap (30 – 60 minutes)

7:00 pm – Feeding

7:30/7:45 pm – Bed

10:00 pm – Dream feed and back to bed

Sample Schedule 8-16 Weeks

(4-hour cycle, dropping the dream feed)

7:00 am – Feeding

8:30/8:45 am – Nap

11:00 am – Feeding

12:30/1:00 pm – Nap (let baby sleep as long as they like)

3:00 pm (or upon waking after 3:00) – Feeding

5:00 pm – Cat Nap (30 – 60 minutes)

6:00 pm – Feeding

7:30/7:45 pm – Optional top off feeding before bed, then bed for the night

Mom – Pump before bed if nursing

4-6 MONTHS: SCHEDULE AND TRANSITIONS

Your baby may need even more awake time at this stage. You can slowly increase awake times by 10-15 minutes at a time, when necessary.

Another transition some babies experience at this stage is adding solids to their diet. Talk to your doctor about starting solids before you begin, just to make sure this is the right timing for your baby and your family. When starting your baby on solids, **always do your liquid feeding first** to make sure the bulk of your baby's intake (calories and nutrition) comes from breast milk or formula, in the first year.

Sample Schedule 4-6 Months
(4-hour cycle and starting solid foods)

7:00 am – Liquid feeding then solids with family at breakfast
9:00 am – Nap
11:00 am – Liquid feeding then solids with family at lunch
1:00 pm – Nap
3:00 pm – Liquid feeding
5:00 pm – Cat nap (30 – 60 minutes)
5:30/6:00 pm – Dinner with family
7:00 pm – Liquid feeding only, then bed

6-9 MONTHS: SCHEDULE AND TRANSITIONS

The biggest factor in transitioning to this age range is the shortening of the morning nap and dropping the late afternoon cat nap. As your baby gets older and gains the ability to handle more awake time, you want to guide your baby toward the afternoon nap.

Why is it important to keep the afternoon nap? A nice, long afternoon nap makes for a pleasant evening with and for the family. If your baby gets a long morning nap, but only a short nap in the afternoon, family time in the evening may be less enjoyable. Babies do tend to prefer the morning nap! So, you must be intentional about keeping the morning nap short and making the afternoon nap longer.

You may notice at any time during this stage that the afternoon nap is getting harder for your baby. It may be harder for him to fall asleep or she may start waking early from the nap. This should serve as an indication that more awake time is necessary for your baby.

Shorten the morning nap on the start side by 15 minutes at a time, until your baby's afternoon nap has returned to a normal length. For example, if your baby typically takes a morning nap from 9:00 am - 11:00 am you will shorten the morning nap by putting baby down later at 9:15 am. Keep in mind that this is a common age to start teething. So, awake time may not be the only reason for inconsistent naps.

> You must be intentional about keeping the morning nap short and the afternoon nap longer.

Your baby will give indicators when it is time to drop the cat nap. If it becomes harder and harder to get your baby to sleep for this nap, or she just refuses to take it, it's time to drop it from the schedule. Bedtime may come slightly earlier, if necessary.

Sample Schedule 6-9 Months
(4-hour cycle and dropping the cat nap)

7:00 am – Liquid feeding then solids with family at breakfast
9:00 am – Nap (may range from 1-2 hour at this point)
11:00 am – Liquid feeding then solids with family at lunch

1:15/1:30 pm – Nap (may range from 2-3 hours)

3:30 pm (or upon waking after 3:30) – Liquid feeding

5:30/6:00 pm – Dinner with family

7:00 pm – Liquid feeding only, then bed (this may be an earlier time if baby has difficulty staying awake until bed)

9-12 MONTHS: SCHEDULE AND TRANSITIONS

During this transition, you will continue to shorten the morning nap until the afternoon nap is still a consistent two to three hours. You will notice that we are no longer following a strict "eat, play, sleep" (EPS) cycle. However, feedings are still not associated with sleep.

The afternoon nap should always be a minimum of two hours, but it can be more if you and your baby desire. Morning naps typically range from 30-90 minutes.

Sample Schedule 9-12 Months
(Transitioning from a 4-hour cycle and guiding baby to afternoon nap)

7:00 am – Liquid feeding and solids with family at breakfast

9:30/10:00 am – Nap (may range from 30 min - 1.5 hrs at this age; make sure nap is over by 11:00 am)

11:30 am – Liquid feeding then solids with family at lunch

1:15/1:30 pm – Nap

4:00 pm - Liquid feeding

5:30/6:00 pm – Dinner with family

7:00 pm – Liquid feeding only

7:30/7:45 pm – Bed

12-18 MONTHS: SCHEDULE AND TRANSITIONS

Many little ones will keep the morning nap beyond a year, but they will typically start the transition process sometime between 13-16 months. If you need to, you can move the afternoon nap to a slightly earlier time for a while, until your toddler can handle more awake time. Gradually move it back in short increments to a comfortable afternoon time.

Many moms choose to wean their babies at or around one year of age. But, if you are still nursing, don't worry, we have a schedule for you, too. The key is this: mom is in control of when nursing happens or doesn't happen.

Sample Schedule 12-18 Months
(Family schedule and short morning nap)

7:00 am – Wake up and breakfast
10:00 am – Nap (20-45 min)
10:45 am – Wake time
12:00 pm – Lunch
1:30 pm – Nap
4:00 pm – Wake time and small snack (handful of cheerios)
5:30 pm – Dinner with family
7:00 pm – Optional sippy cup of milk
7:30/7:45 pm – Bed

Sample Schedule 12-18 Months
(Family schedule and dropping the morning nap)

7:00 am – Wake up and breakfast
12:00 pm – Lunch
12:30/1:30 pm – Nap
3:00/4:00 pm – Wake time and small snack (handful of cheerios)
5:30 pm – Dinner with family
7:00 pm – Optional sippy cup of milk
7:30/7:45 pm – Bed

Sample Schedule 12-18 Months
(Family schedule with nursing)

7:00 am – Nursing then breakfast with family
10:00 am – Possible nap (20-45 min)
10:45 am – Wake time and nursing
12:00 pm – Lunch
12:30/1:30 pm – Nap
3:00/4:00 pm – Wake time and nursing
5:30 pm – Dinner with family
7:00 pm – Nursing
7:30/7:45 pm – Bed

18 MONTHS TO 3 YEARS: SCHEDULE AND TRANSITIONS

Not much changes, here, for quite some time. Your toddler will have a consistent afternoon nap for the next couple years. I bet that sounds great! When she reaches three years old, you may need to shorten the nap, little-by-little. But don't get too antsy to make it too short or drop it completely. Fill your morning time with plenty of structured activities, learning, and play.

Sample Schedule 18 Months - 3 Years
7:00 am – Wake up and breakfast
12:00 pm – Lunch
1:30 pm – Nap
4:00 pm – Wake time and small snack
5:30 pm – Dinner with family
7:00 pm – Bedtime routine
7:45/8:00 pm – Bed

Well, there you have it. You now have the basic information you need to set up the appropriate schedules for your baby, from infancy up to three years old. Now let's do some fine tweaking.

 **Alicia Westphal**
8 hours ago · 🖼

When he was first born, I thought our baby would "tell" us when he was ready to sleep every day. Surprise! He did not. My Baby Can Sleep's schedule & advice rescued us from ourselves. He's now so predictable, healthy, & happy. We've even been able to work at home this year thanks to his schedule. We couldn't have done it without MBCS!

Amanda Abernathy   · · ·
1 hour ago ·

My husband and I thrive off of schedules so it only makes sense our baby boy would too! We were clueless first time parents begging for help. MBCS saved us. Through mentor calls with Greta she guided us in finding the right schedule for Derek to get us all sleeping again! Once we had the schedule in place, we were all thriving and still are today! — with **Ryan Abernathy**.

 3

Kellie Walker
18 mins · 👥

•••

The concept of a schedule was foreign to me as a new mother. When I had my daughter, I was told she will eat when she is hungry and she will sleep when she is tired. I quickly realized that wasn't the case! I am so thankful that the My Baby Can Sleep Sleep Accelerator Course had a schedule to follow at each stage during my babies development! When we got her on a schedule, everything changed for the better!

👍 Like   💬 Comment

118

Chapter Eight

FINE TWEAKING

This is the last chapter with me (Greta), and then Brad will take you the rest of the way home.

You've completed your sleep training, implemented a successful daytime routine, eliminated any and all of your baby's sleep crutches, and your baby is sleeping through the night. Life is good! And then it happens. Seemingly out of nowhere, your baby starts waking up at night again. Your baby has gone from not needing a feeding after bed time to now wanting two feedings in the night. Or, maybe your baby is sleeping through the night, but naps have gone from perfect to terrible.

In this chapter we're going talk about the reasons why some babies regress in their sleep training.

DON'T QUIT!

If your baby experiences a regression in his well-trained sleep habits, you may be tempted to throw in the towel—Don't quit! Don't give up! Don't go back to accepting your baby's frequent nighttime waking as a normal way of life.

As you know, babies change as they grow. Sometimes a little fine tweaking in your schedule or some other aspect of sleep training is necessary to put your baby back into rhythm. The good news is that just as our sleep training method works, so do the tweaks you can implement along the way.

THE THREE REASONS FOR SLEEP REGRESSION

There are three primary reasons under which most, if not all, forms of sleep regression fall. The first is that your baby is experiencing a developmental change. The second is due to unusual circumstances (i.e. teething, illness, change of bed, etc.). The third is that mom and dad are failing to stick to the schedule, or are falling back into old habits.

DEVELOPMENTAL CHANGES

As babies grow they need more awake time and less sleep time. By way of reminder: remember that you want to guide your baby toward afternoon naps.

If, for instance, your baby is struggling with sleep during naptime, then simply shorten the morning naptime in short increments—only 15 minutes at a time. If your baby continues to struggle, simply decrease the naptime by another 15 minutes (a little longer or a little shorter, depending on your specific circumstances). Continue to do so until your baby's afternoon naptime sleep returns to normal.

The disruption in your baby's sleep could be due to insufficient calorie intake during the day. As your baby develops, he is going to need more calories to sustain his energy level. This can be accomplished by either adding an additional feeding (bottle or nursing), or adding additional ounces to the feedings already in place. (Most breastfeeding moms find that their milk supply adjusts naturally along with baby's needs, and no change in feeding schedule is necessary). It could be that your baby has reached the stage in his development that indicates it's time to start adding solids to his diet. If you decide to add an additional feeding, place that new feeding sometime before your baby's morning or afternoon nap. And a word of caution: make sure not to allow the additional feedings to become a sleep crutch for your baby.

I do want to make you aware of the "four-month sleep regression," a stage that is well-known in the baby sleep training community. I refer to it instead as a four-month developmental change.

Your baby's fourth month of life is a dramatic time of transition. Your baby is waking up, truly becoming aware of the world around him. Your baby is fascinated by what he now sees and hears, and he doesn't want to miss a thing!

If your baby experiences a disruption in sleep during this four-month stage, the simplest solution is to power through the disruption by sticking to your schedule. Don't deviate from the good work you are doing. If there are aspects of training you have stopped because baby had been sleeping so well, such as the 45-minute timer, simply re-introduce those back into your schedule to help get back on track. Your baby will likely protest, but that's okay and to be expected. The good news is that if you remain consistent, usually after about a week or so, your baby will settle back into his sleep routine.

> I refer to it instead as a four-month developmental change.

UNUSUAL CIRCUMSTANCES

Now, let's talk about unusual circumstances that might disrupt your baby's sleep. Experiences like teething or catching a cold can disrupt a baby's sleep.

The most painful part of teething usually lasts only a day or two, maybe up to a week. How long teething pain lasts is determined, in large part, to how many teeth are trying to break through at the time. Your baby's 12 to 15-month molars may take longer than his other teeth to break through the gums. Molar teething can also be more painful than with your baby's other teeth.

Do whatever you would typically do to manage your baby's teething pain, whether that's pain medication or a natural remedy.

Illness can also disrupt your baby's good sleep habits. As with teething, illness is a time to focus on meeting your baby's physical needs. You can wait until your baby is well again before re-implementing aspects of his sleep training to get him back on track.

You may need to offer your baby more frequent and shorter feedings. If your baby is congested, it will be difficult for him to get the good, full feeding he needs. By implementing extra feedings, you can compensate for calories lost during the shorter-due-to-illness feedings during the day.

> Sleep-trained babies tend to sleep better during time of illness, and therefore, may recover more quickly.

When your baby is ill, you may have to hold him for an extended period of time. It's all right to have your baby sleep in your arms in order to comfort or simply prop up your baby while he is ill. If your baby forms any bad habits because of an altered schedule or routine due to illness, you can always re-implement sleep training for as long as necessary, after your baby recovers from his illness.

This should encourage you. Sleep-trained babies tend to sleep better during time of illness (and therefore, may recover more quickly) than babies who have never been sleep trained.

Sometimes the unusual circumstance is nothing more than a bad night's sleep. Maybe your baby experiences a nightmare. Maybe they are too hot or too cold to get comfortable. Or, maybe a poor night's sleep is simply unexplainable. If you're desperate and have no clue what to do, make sure you are wise in how you respond. We want to make sure we are meeting baby's needs, not necessarily his wants.

Sometimes, all it takes is for baby to receive one middle-of-the-night feeding for him to quickly fall back into those habits that prevented him from sleeping in the first place. So, you want to be very cautious before going back to offering your baby a middle-of-the-night-feeding. Before you do so, ask yourself: "Am I meeting my baby's needs? Does he just need comfort at this time, or does he really need the intake of calories?"

PARENTS RETURNING TO OLD HABITS

There are times when your baby's sleep schedule could be disrupted because either you, or your spouse, or both of you have slipped back into the old habits you recently eliminated. To determine that, let me ask you a series of questions:

1. Are you characterized by naps on the go? Does your

baby sleep more in your car than in his own bed?

2. Are you inconsistent about your start time each day? Are you getting your baby up beyond that 30-minute flexibility, which we discussed in Chapter Seven?

3. Are you going back to old habits—the habits you've worked so hard to break (i.e. rocking or nursing your baby back to sleep, or bringing your baby into bed with you)?

Do any of the above questions describe you and/or your current situation? If so, correct and discipline yourself to go back to the basics. Some people struggle with being too strict; while others struggle with being too flexible when it comes to their baby's sleep training. Remember: consistency is key, and you want to avoid any and all extremes. You don't want to be "too" anything when it comes to your baby's sleep training. Be wise. Be structured. Be consistent.

Don't get discouraged. If you are struggling with falling back into bad habits, you're not alone. There are many people like you. Remember: Brad and I were just like you before we discovered, implemented, and started teaching baby sleep training. It could be argued that Brad and I struggled with consistency worse than most. We thought ourselves so prepared and so educated, only to realize we were *clueless!*

What Brad and I needed when we struggled with consistency was support. This is just another reason why we are so passionate about supporting you!

Brad's going to be leading you through these final chapters. He's going to inspire you to get your baby and yourself sleeping and to not fall back into bad habits. We want you to have a healthy baby and a healthy family, which includes healthy sleep habits for you and your loved ones.

CHAPTER 8
TAKE AWAYS

- Sleep regressions happen. Identifying the cause is the first step in correcting the problem.

- The three reasons and solutions are:

  - Developmental changes - simply adjust the schedule in small amounts until nights and afternoon naps return to normal.

  - Teething or illness - work with your baby as much as possible to meet his needs, giving medication or natural remedies if necessary. When your baby is well it may be necessary to retrain any bad habits that were developed during the time of illness.

  - Backsliding - get back to the basics. Commit to the basics of training again and get motivated to make it happen!

Andrea Hickey   ・・・

When we were thinking about sleep training, we had SO MANY questions and no one to really ask. We found **#mybabycansleep** and have never looked back! The thing that stood out to us the most was the ongoing mentorship through the process and beyond. We are so grateful for the continuous support; it has made all the difference.

Hope Crowe Dawson
8 hours ago · 🖼

Our son hit his 4 month sleep regression hard and we thought we'd never get a full nights sleep again until we found MBCS! Brad and Greta have been life savors mentoring us on how to adjust his schedule when needed and now we handle situations with a sound mind knowing MBCS is always there when we need them!

👍 Jaclyn Fuller and 7 others

👍 Like   💬 Comment

Jaclyn Fuller   · · ·

My kids have always been late risers since birth. When I had our second child I still had no idea what it meant to sleep train. I tried following books that said what a "typical" schedule was for my babies age. It always backfired since my baby didn't wake at the right time. Finally at 6 months when my baby wasn't napping at all and was taking hours to go to sleep at night I was desperate for help. I purchased the sleep accelerator course without discussing with my husband because I was so desperate for sleep. I learned I was using the EPS routine backwards and was feeding on demand. With the help of Greta and figuring out a new schedule my baby in face could sleep. Thanks to MBCS we are due to have our third child in April which I never thought would be possible due to sleep issues my first two had. — with **Patrick Fuller**.

Chapter Nine

THE SECRET SAUCE

Thus far, you have been guided through this extraordinary process by my amazing wife, Greta. Obviously I'm a little partial because I married her, but she is absolutely fabulous at everything she does, including getting babies to sleep through the night. I (Brad) am going to take you the rest of the way. We're going to spend the last couple chapters getting you excited, motivated, and as ready as you can be to get started.

In this chapter, I want to talk about what I call the "secret sauce."

THERE WE WERE

There we were, sitting in a parenting class, before we were even pregnant with our first child. Greta and I had big plans. We were going to be smart; we were going to be ahead of others in this baby-raising game. We were going to be the golden couple—the new parents that other parents looked to as the example.

Then, reality invaded our optimism. Along came our baby and she didn't sleep through the night. It was actually a dark and trying time in our life and in our marriage. We were tired, frustrated, embarrassed, and we just wanted someone to tell us what to do to get our baby to sleep. We hadn't taken into account the tiredness and fatigue that come with a new baby, which made us unable to think clearly on all that knowledge we amassed.

The moral of our story is that information alone is not enough. It was our personal experience that sparked the MyBabyCanSleep concept.

There are so many sleep consultants out there that simply sell information. Now, at hearing that, I bet you're thinking, "Brad, I just read eight chapters of your book. And now you're telling me information is not enough?" Well, the reality for most parents is that information alone is simply not enough. What's needed and what's missing in most baby sleep methods (and what Greta and I are bringing to transform the baby sleep industry), is the emotional and mental support to correctly and consistently apply all the things you've learned about to get baby sleeping through the night.

Look: I can sit down and put together what I consider to be a fabulous workout plan. However, the key to actually getting it done is having the discipline to set the alarm each day, get out of bed, get dressed, leave the house, and go to the gym! Most people think the treadmill is what will help you lose weight. Although it might be a required piece of equipment it's the act of getting on the treadmill and using it routinely that becomes the real 'it' factor. And sometimes, in order to put the plan to work, we need accountability. We need a partner. We need someone who will work with us and encourage us to take the plan from paper (information) to fruition (actually doing it). Remember: Information is NOT transformation!

We like to use the following example with our clients. It's like buying a book on Spanish, and expecting to be fluent in Spanish, after a couple days of reading. I think you would agree that it is an unrealistic expectation. So, I want to assure you that you didn't waste your money on our book. This book is a really good (and necessary) starting point for what you're trying to accomplish.

> Remember: Information is NOT transformation!

In our story, Greta and I were way too tired and stressed out. We were too close to the situation. It's why lawyers don't defend their own children in court. It's why surgeons don't operate on their own family. We were so deeply involved in the details that we just couldn't see the forest for the trees.

YOU'VE TRIED EVERYTHING

I want you to think about this statement: if you could have gotten your baby sleeping on your own you probably would have done so by now. Make sense? Greta and I know, from our own experience, you've probably tried everything you could think of to solve the problem yourself. And we know that you're reading this book because you realized you need help. It's no small thing to us that you would turn to us for help. Again, this is why we are so passionate and so committed to providing you with the help you need—the kind of help we know works. The kind that goes far and above just handing you information and sending you on your way, with only hope as your game plan.

Greta and I know this book has provided you with tons of information.. But now, maybe you're sitting there with our book in your hand, thinking, "I've got the information. In fact, I *understand* the information you've given me. But I'm struggling with the follow-through. I'm struggling with implementing everything I've just learned. I need more help..."

GOING ABOVE AND BEYOND

Here's where we're going to go above and beyond. This book is more than a book. This book is a ticket, a passport, into a community. Greta and I want to cordially invite you to join our free, public, sleep help group on Facebook. You can either go to Facebook and type "MyBabyCanSleep" in the search bar, or simply go to MyBabyCanSleep.com/BookGroup to join for free.

By joining our free group, you will be linked to literally thousands of moms, from around the world who are all just like you: ready for sleep! Greta and I spend time daily, via live video or chat inside the group along with our paid team to help answer questions and guide you in putting the pieces together. Again, the reason for this is that we know that providing tangible, emotional and mental support is the key to the success of MyBabyCanSleep. And again, we know how hard it is to do this alone. We understand that anything in life, whether it's quitting smoking or getting your baby to sleep, it's always easier to accomplish the goal when you are part of a group of people all working to accomplish the same thing.

This book is a ticket, a passport, into a community.

And that, my friends, is the secret sauce. Real community. Actual support. Genuine care. A community to answer your ongoing questions.

THE ONLY THING HARDER THAN SLEEP TRAINING

So, if after reading this book you are feeling overwhelmed, here's one of the key takeaways: The only thing harder than sleep training your baby is *not* sleep training your baby. This bears repeating: The only thing harder than sleep training

135

your baby is *not* sleep training your baby. What you've been doing and what you've been experiencing is probably the hardest way to do things. You've been trying to get your baby to sleep without a clear path, without a clear plan, and without any emotional or mental support.

> The only thing harder than sleep training your baby is **not** sleep training your baby.

You've been doing it alone, and you've been doing it fatigued. What I just described is probably the worst possible way to accomplish anything in life, let alone getting a baby sleeping through the night.

Greta and I speak with moms, dads, and families every single day. Not a day goes by that I don't speak to a family either on the phone or on the website chat where I don't spend upward of 80% of our time simply providing emotional support, letting moms know this is normal, they are normal, and their babies are normal. Greta and I spend most of our time simply being available to people and reassuring them that what they're experiencing is both normal and common. So even if you think you're one that knows what to do, the simple comfort of knowing someone is there makes all the difference in the world. We gladly and enthusiastically spend much of our time reassuring moms and dads that they can do it, that they can get their babies to sleep through the night. Again, most sleep consultants spend one, maybe two times actually interacting with their clients. Our ongoing mentorship model is not found anywhere else!

THIS IS A LIFESTYLE

You see; MyBabyCanSleep is more than just a program or a method. It's a lifestyle. This isn't like a fad diet. True dieting involves a healthy lifestyle of eating and exercise that sustains. Being a great parent, being a great spouse, and getting your baby sleeping through the night is a way of life. This is why we want you to join our free community and come experience the MyBabyCanSleep lifestyle at www.MyBabyCanSleep.com/BookGroup.

One of the great things about what we do is that Greta and I are a husband and wife team. There are very few, if any other, husband and wife teams in the baby sleep consultant field. One of the neat things for me, as a dad, is that I know how to get other dads on board. I enjoy helping them to be more communicative with their wives about the struggle of having a baby that is not sleeping, and encourage them as they work toward getting their babies to sleep through the night. Getting dads on board is critically important to putting moms and dads on the same page and working together toward the same goal. Yes, it's great to have an online community like ours

> Join our free online community for book buyers at www.mybabycansleep.com/bookgroup

for support, but having the cooperation of both parents in a two-parent family is invaluable for the emotional and mental support of both parents.

Besides sleep, one of the many things we focus on at MyBabyCanSleep is the importance of date nights for parents. The mommy-daddy relationship is vital to the success of a family, let alone the success of getting your baby to sleep through the night. We encourage all of our married couples to go on dates as frequently as possible and at least once per month. We also encourage our couples to go on quarterly overnights to just get away and focus on their marriages, which is the foundation of the family unit. This doesn't always happen perfectly but our students show dramatic increases in these activities when surrounded by others who make it a priority as well. Focusing on the marriage relationship is critical so that moms and dads can have the energy, the motivation, and the necessary rest to put the time and effort into being a great spouse and parent. So if your last date night was many months ago, you're long overdue for spending time on your marriage and we'll help you make it happen on a much more regular basis.

Remember: the only thing harder than sleep training your baby is not sleep training your baby. So, again, please don't try to do this on your own. There's no merit badge; there are no extra brownie points for making this journey alone. Save the "do-it-yourself" projects for Pinterest and Home Depot. Don't do it with your baby's sleep. Become part of a community that's laser-focused on one plan that will help you streamline your effort to get baby sleeping through the night.

Here's the bottom line. Old habits are really hard to break. It's one of the hardest things we, as humans, try to do. The older we get, the older and more ingrained our bad habits are, the more difficult it is to break them. That's why we need the help of others who have "been there, and done that" to help us crush those bad habits so they never return. If you don't have a plan to break the old habits, they'll never accidentally nor magically become unbroken.

> Save the "do-it-yourself" projects for your backyard, the garage, or a home remodel.

BEFORE WE TURN YOU LOOSE

So, we've got one more chapter to go. This next chapter is arguably one of, if not the most important chapters in the book. I know you're more than ready to get your baby sleeping through the night. And I hope you're as excited as we are to get started. But before we turn you loose, I want to show you exactly how we work with families in our program, our Sleep Accelerator Course that the baby world can't stop talking about.

Maybe you're a family that says, "We need this. We need all of it—the training, the emotional and mental support; I want to have guaranteed results that our baby will sleep through the night. I don't want to do it alone; I want to get my questions answered." If you're wanting to take everything to the next level, then stay with me. What we are going to cover in the next chapter is your ticket to *guaranteed* baby sleep.

Greta and I are unashamedly confident that we are the couple to provide you with the best possible help. Our program is so amazing that we actually guarantee that it will work for your family.

Turn the page and learn how you can join our Sleep Accelerator Course. After all...investing in your family is the best investment you can make!

Amy Torres
3 minutes ago · 🖼

When Ben was born in 2016, we had no idea what
we were doing sleep-wise, and Greta's reassuring
guidance got him sleeping on a schedule. But
really, we needed you and this community every
step of the way. You gave us the knowledge and
support through every sleep change as he grew.
Now he's two and still sleeping like a champ!

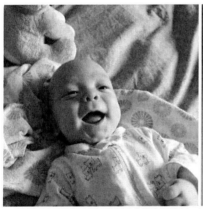

👍 Like   💬 Comment

Cherish Leigh Roberts
Fri at 3:35 PM · 🖼

Nap times have been night and day different for our family with the help of MBCS. The fact that my baby can sleep anywhere allows me to feel the freedom to spend time with God, visit with friends, and take care of the chores. All this allows me to be a better wife and momma! This is only possible because of MBCS!

Elizabeth Villwock
Yesterday at 10:51 PM ·

The community Brad & Greta have cultivated at My Baby Can Sleep is unlike any other group I've been a part of. The group has been an incredible support system not only as we have trained both of our kids how to sleep, but also as we have continued to figure out this whole parenting thing with 2 under 2.

🔼 You, Jaclyn Fuller and 6 others

 Like   💬 Comment

Chapter Ten

SLEEP ACCELERATOR COURSE

All right. You've now reached the last chapter of the book. In this chapter we will focus our attention on explaining to you our Sleep Accelerator Course. Purchasing this additional course gives you the opportunity to work directly with us and get *guaranteed* baby sleep. If you want to take the next step and join Greta and I along with 1,000+ other families all over the world in our Sleep Accelerator Course, we want to make sure we give you all of the details you need.

You really don't want to skip a single word in this chapter because what we do is very unique. In order to make sure you glean everything you need, I want to begin by providing some background regarding the baby sleep consulting industry.

THE BABY SLEEP CONSULTING INDUSTRY

Back to our story. When we discovered that the key—the

"secret sauce" to success is receiving and providing emotional and mental support to parents, we began searching for other programs that provided the same. What we quickly discovered was that no one else offered long-term ongoing support. We were amazed by how quickly our offer to provide not only information, but complete mentoring and intimate continual support practically went viral.

In our research, we found that 99% of the consultants in this field charge between $300 and $500 for a one-time, one-hour phone call. If you're fortunate, you might receive one or two follow-up emails after the phone call. However, more often than not, your money simply buys you a one-hour phone call.

Needless to say, Greta and I strongly disagree with that model. We knew right away that investing in that kind of support, or lack thereof, was not going to get us the results our family desperately needed. It's all about the *ongoing* emotional and mental support. After you hang up the phone from a one-time call with most other consultants, you'll

> After you hang up the phone from a one-time call with most other consultants, you'll have nothing left but hope as a strategy.

have nothing left but *hope* as a strategy. Just as one shower won't keep a person clean all week, one phone call wouldn't be enough to keep us on track, motivated, and consistent in the necessary work to help our baby sleep through the night (and not to mention the many changes and transitions you will need help with along the way). Remember...information alone is not enough!

OUR THREE-TIERED SYSTEM

Greta and I have developed a three-tiered system for our Sleep Accelerator Course. The first tier is information. While providing information is only about 20% of what we do, we understand how important it is for you to have the *right* information. We believe, as we've shown in this book, that we provide the best possible information for you to successfully get your baby to sleep through the night, as quickly as possible.

The second tier of our three-tier system is community. A community laughs together, cries together, encourages each other through struggles, and rejoices in each other's successes on a daily basis. The encouragement of a like-minded community is an invaluable resource to help you accomplish your parenting goals.

The third tier of our three-tier system is providing you with support—a direct pipeline for getting answers to your questions by us. As you likely already know, a baby's needs change as he or she grows. Those needs can change rapidly, sometimes daily, especially when the baby is very young. Herein lies the problem with most books on this topic. How many babies go "by the book?" What do you do if your baby doesn't fit into the cookie cutter mold that the book provides? The chances of you winning the lottery are probably greater than the chances of your baby going "by the book" through their entire infancy. Every family is unique and every baby is unique. We will provide you with an expert evaluation and plan customized for your situation.

There you have it, our three-tiered system: information, community, and support.

Having read this book, you have a solid foundation in the 'information tier' of our three-tiered model. Now, you're ready to join our community, having already learned the language. You're ready to communicate with other parents who are either right where you are on the journey, or who have already been there. Most importantly, you're ready to communicate with Greta and I. We can do that extremely effectively by diving into your life to make the small tweaks that make all the difference in the world, since we won't have to spend our time on the basics taught in our book. You're already much closer to baby sleep than you think!

> The chances of you winning the lottery are probably greater than the chances of your baby going "by the book" through their entire infancy.

HERE'S WHAT YOU GET

Now we are ready to outline exactly what you get by joining our Sleep Accelerator Course. This is really exciting!

The first thing you get when your join our program is <u>lifetime</u> access to our members' area videos. We believe that it is important to provide you with information in a video format. We want you to see our faces and hear our voices, and we know many people learn better through listening. This allows for 15-20 times the amount of training you receive compared to the one-hour phone call model.

Mom, let's be honest. Your husband may not be too keen on reading a 250-page book. He's probably not going to read a book even as short as this one. Not that he can't, but rather he likely may not have the time or the interest. One of the most important reasons for providing information via video is to help you and your husband get on the same page. We believe the quickest and easiest way to do that is by providing short videos that you and your husband can watch together.

We presently have more than 100 videos that take you step-by-step through the process. These videos cover baby ages from newborn to three years old (and beyond). And they address a variety of topics: teething, swaddling, what to do when your baby poops in the middle of the night, napping, dream feeding, and much more. But don't worry, you don't have to watch all 100! The videos are all à la carte as well, so you go right to the videos you need. Just about every situation and possibility, drawn from our own experience raising seven children, is addressed in our videos. Greta and I are committed to giving you the fullest possible picture of what life may be like, from the moment your baby is born through the first few years of his or her life.

Remember that community we talked about? As part of our second tier of our three-tier system you gain lifetime access to our supportive, encouraging, student-only "Mastermind" Facebook community of parents who are all trying to accomplish what you are and who are all doing it the same way (yes, this is different from our free community we spoke about in Chapter Nine). We know there are a lot of online communities out there. But most of them are comprised of 60,000 moms giving 60,000 different ideas for solving one problem. The online community we have developed is laser-focused, motivated, and on the same page. While there are many voices in our community (honest communication is key), the voices are not competing with one another. This is what makes our online community unique. You will join the conversation with 1,000+ moms who are discussing the MyBabyCanSleep methods to overcome the same challenges, and using the same tools to solve similar problems.

Many of these moms will have the same experience level as you. You will also be able to draw from the wisdom of moms who have children months or years older than your own, and who have been through exactly what you are going through at this stage with your baby. Again, the moms you meet in this very special Mastermind community will be operating from the same playbook, so everyone is on the same page.

Not only will like-minded moms be there to support you and give you encouragement along the way, Greta and I, along with our paid staff of consultants, will get your questions answered here quickly! What's great about this access is that you can literally ask us an unlimited amount of questions inside the group....forever. This is how we join you on the journey and provide ongoing mentorship to ensure sleep happens. No expirations and no pressure of only being able to use a certain number of lifelines. We have students who joined our program two years ago that still can ask us questions!

The third, most amazing part of the program is that direct pipeline to us! Greta and I are giving you four, yes four, group mentoring sessions to use to speak with us "face to face" on webcam. You will be able to log on and join us with a few other moms for live, real-time, mentoring to talk through any major issues you may have, or even just get a little boost of encouragement straight from Greta herself! There is no pressure to use these four calls within a certain time period and most only use two as baby sleep comes so fast with our method. Which brings me to the bonuses.

FAMILY PASS BONUS

By joining our Sleep Accelerator Program through the link

we'll give you, you'll also get our Family Pass Bonus free! The Family Pass means we will let you ask sleep questions about *all* of your children. Remember that one-time, one-hour phone call for which other sleep consultants charge $300 to $500 for? Well that can be the cost *per child*. Don't think you're going to have a second baby? Trust me...when we get them sleeping so easily, you might just have energy for another!

Obviously, you can see that the design of our three-tier model is far superior just one call or one email you get with others. Greta and I believe in and are committed to providing you with the ongoing support you need. We are with you every step of the way, during your journey, to ensure your success. There are no time limits to our support. There are no expiration dates to our services.

TODDLER BEHAVIOR MINI COURSE BONUS

Greta and I are also toddler behavior experts and have a completely separate and equally amazing toddler behavior course that starts with babies as young as nine months with basic high chair manners, meal time challenges, sharing, hitting, and other behavioral issues. Although this course is separate, we are going to include a miniature version of the course inside the Sleep Accelerator Course. Basically, we've taken about a dozen of the top videos from the Toddler Course and are giving them to you FREE along with the Sleep Accelerator Course when you join. If you just had or are going to have your first baby I can promise you the need for these videos will come much sooner than you think!

REFERRAL BONUS PROGRAM

So when you join the program and get your baby sleeping fast, you're going to be excited to tell your friends, family, and strangers at the grocery store how amazing our system is and naturally be bringing new people into the program. We won't let this go unnoticed! We will give you instant qualification into our referral program. If you choose to encourage others and they decide to join, you'll get paid as a "thank you" from us. Pretty simple. Many of our students have received enough referral bonuses that they've easily paid for the program over and over again.

COURSE RECAP

Let's recap quickly exactly what you're going to get:

- Lifetime access to our members' area videos
- Lifetime access to our Facebook Mastermind Group
- Four group mentor sessions with us on webcam
- Our Family Pass Bonus
- The Toddler Behavior Mini Course Bonus
- Qualification for our referral bonus program

Here's what we recommend doing next.

NEXT STEPS

So, here are more details about the Sleep Accelerator Program and the practical steps to getting started.

First, sign-up for our Sleep Accelerator Course www. MyBabyCanSleep.com/SignUp . You'll create your username and password. Then, you can start watching the online videos immediately. Remember that I said we have over 100 videos? Well, most moms only need to watch five or six videos that pertain to their baby's specific age, in order to get started. They can then reference other topical videos as those issues arise. Of course, again, as part of our Sleep Accelerator Course, you will have lifetime access to all of the videos. So, you can watch the videos you need whenever you need.

Second, click the link to inside the video course to request access to our private, student-only Mastermind group. You will be welcomed in so you can start asking questions right away.

Third, whenever you have a need that requires a bit more counsel, go to the events tab inside the Mastermind group to see when the next mentor session will be held and RSVP.

THE BEST PART

Now, for the best part! At MyBabyCanSleep, we have an action-based guarantee. We guarantee to get your baby sleeping through the night (seven to eight hours), in 30 days or less (or by 12 weeks of age, whichever comes second), or we will gladly provide you with a refund. However, just as you expect us to be good teachers, we expect you to be a good student as well. You have to be willing to follow our lead. We need you to post your questions in the Mastermind Facebook group and participate in all of your mentoring sessions. We also would like you to fill out a daily sleep training evaluation form, which is provided in our course downloads.

That being said and understood, we are so confident in the system we've designed and the support we provide, that if you follow through and for some reason you don't get your baby sleeping through the night, we will refund you the entire cost of the program.

Since we've begun offering our action-based sleep guarantee, we have not had to issue a single refund!

This isn't guesswork. Greta and I have experience helping parents with babies of all ages, in all kinds of families; this includes, twins, triplets, babies born premature, babies with autism, Down syndrome and everything in between. Your situation may feel unique to you but it is not unique to us! We've seen and done it all and then some.

As Greta mentioned earlier, babies eight weeks and older generally are able to sleep eight hours through the night within about one week of training—sometimes, sleep happens within just a few days. We are going to help you achieve results that are quite literally life changing and get you back to your normal rested self, enjoying your family and your marriage!

Lack of sleep affects every aspect of life. Lack of sleep affects every relationship in the home, not the least of which is the relationship between mom and dad. It affects your work. It affects your health. We encourage you—we plead with you— if your baby is not sleeping, get help. Get help now. Let Greta and I, along with our amazing team, help you. Investing in your baby's sleep is one of the most important investments you can make.

AN IMPORTANT DECISION

You now have a very important decision to make. You can do one of two things: You can continue to do what you've been doing with your baby and struggle with inconsistent, sporadic sleep each night. You can continue doing it alone, the hard way.

OR... you can dramatically change course and get real sleep real fast. You can choose to get the emotional and mental support to compliment the information you've received in this book, and get your baby sleeping through the night.

If you're ready to make this happen, go to MyBabyCanSleep. com/SignUp and join our Sleep Accelerator Course.
There's one last thing I want you to do. You see, when you join

MyBabyCanSleep, you are embracing a new lifestyle. The old is gone, the new has come. I want you to read the following manifesto very carefully, and let it sink in. We encourage our students to post this where they can see it—in their nursery, car, on the refrigerator—to keep them motivated in their efforts. Let this become your manifesto as well:

I am now a courageous and confident parent
who is finally going to stand against
not sleeping and not napping.
I love my child so much that I now fully understand
that they must be taught how and when to sleep.

I'm done making excuses and I can't believe
that I put up with no sleep for this long.
I realize that the only thing harder than sleep training
my baby is not sleep training my baby—
that I'll either pay now or pay much more later,
and doing life the way I currently know it
is no longer an option.

I am no longer alone, anxious, or confused.
I now have direct access to one of the leading sleep
consultants in the world, and a community full of
people just like me that have my back.

I'm now in control and have a clear path
to the finish line.

I have everything and everyone required

to get me there.

It won't be a walk in the park but it will be worth it because my marriage and family will no longer suffer; my mental and physical health will no longer suffer.

My feet are on a firm foundation.
My baby can sleep!

Greta and I are really looking forward to working with you inside our Sleep Accelerator Course.

MyBabyCanSleep.com/SignUp

 **Katelyn Voelkel**
12 minutes ago · 🖼

The MBCS Sleep Accelerator Course is the best program we found during our LONG search for a plan to help our baby sleep. The online training videos are so clear and really gave us all the information we needed to be successful, but they didn't stop there. The community that continues to support us throughout transitions with our first and training baby number two has been exactly what every other program was lacking. We are so thankful to Brad and Greta and My Baby Can Sleep for getting both our babies sleeping. We feel much better equipped to parent two under two now that we are all well rested!

Liz Pirtle
32 minutes ago · 🖼️

When we found My Baby Can Sleep we were exhausted, frustrated, overwhelmed, & felt like we were failing as parents. This program was the best parenting decision we've made! We not only gained great parenting knowledge, but we also gained a peace of mind that our baby is happy and rested.

👍 2

    👍 Like   💬 Comment

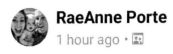

RaeAnne Porte

1 hour ago · 🖼

· · ·

When my husband and I found out at birth that our son Rockton has Down syndrome, to say we were overwhelmed was an understatement. I just so happened to stumble on Brad and Greta when Rockton was 8 weeks old, after a completely sleepless weekend (literally)! At first I was leery this program would help our guy out considering some of his complexities, but we were desperate. 😊 It proved to be LIFE CHANGING! The program not only got Rockton sleeping, but it helped Jake and I as parents understand babies and the right philosophy of parenting. I highly recommend this program to anyone who has children with special needs, because they may have to work extra hard in some areas (breastfeeding for example) which means that sleep is that much more important! We attribute Rockton's vibrant life now at 1 1/2 in part to Brad and Greta's program!